THE KABBALAH METHOD

The Bridge Between Science and The Soul, Physics
and Fulfillment, Quantum and The Creator

THE KABBALAH METHOD

The Bridge Between Science and The Soul, Physics and Fulfillment, Quantum and The Creator

FROM THE TEACHINGS OF KABBALIST RAV BERG   www.kabbalah.com™

For further information:

The Kabbalah Centre
155 E. 48th St., New York, NY 10017
1062 S. Robertson Blvd., Los Angeles, CA 90035

1.800.Kabbalah
www.kabbalah.com

First Edition, January 2005
Printed in USA
ISBN 1-57189-246-x

Table of Contents

The Kabbalah Method

INTRODUCTION

The soul is speaking to the Creator: "Teach me the mysteries of the higher wisdom. How do you lead your flock in the upper world? Teach me so that I will not be shamed when I arrive among the eternal souls, for until now I have not reflected on these mysteries."

The Creator replies to the soul: "If you don't understand the beauty of the soul — if you return and haven't reflected on the wisdom before you came here and don't know anything of the mysteries of the upper world — then you aren't merited to enter here. Therefore, return again. Study those things that people consider to be unimportant. Learn the secrets of the upper world."

Zohar Hadash, Song of Songs
p. 70, sec. 4

We are born into this mysterious universe without a guidebook or an instruction manual. We have only our instincts, our intuition, and our reason to tell us where we came from, why we are here, and what we are supposed to do. But the most important thing we possess — and perhaps the key to our survival as a species — is an almost unlimited need to know. A human being comes into this world with a passionate sense of wonder and inquisitiveness and an equally powerful need for self-expression.

Over the centuries, humankind has gained deep and penetrating insights into the "how" of things, but we have made scant headway into the "why." Despite our many stunning achievements, are we any closer to uncovering answers to the ultimate questions? Have we any greater understanding of the essence of our existence than did the First Man and the First Woman, when they gazed awestruck into a clear, starry sky and contemplated the Great Mystery?

Who are we? Where did we come from? Why are we here? Why did the universe come into being? Did life on earth emerge as a matter of chance, or was it the conscious act of a supreme being? Is our suffering a cruel hoax, or is it a constituent element of some grand design?

Despite all our best efforts to arrive at a conclusive understanding of reality, the essential questions concerning the nature of existence remain impenetrable. That in itself is not particularly alarming. What is unsettling is that today, perhaps as in no other time in history, we are failing as individuals to meet the challenge to probe life's mysteries. We no longer feel comfortable attempting to answer the essential questions. We have grown meek, surrendering the investigation to so-called specialists, consultants, experts, and professionals.

Open to me an opening no bigger than the eye of a needle, and I will open to you the supernal gates.

Zohar III, p. 95a

The most powerful computer ever invented is not locked in some massive government vault, nor is it the jealously guarded secret of any corporate giant. No, the most advanced computer ever created is a strange-looking thing that weighs no more than a few pounds, a convoluted mass of tissue known as the human brain.

"Then why," you might ask, "can't I tap into the infinite potential of this intelligence? Why can't I answer all the questions that have never been answered? Why can't I make the world over exactly as I want it to be?"

Why, indeed! The truth is, the sum total of current human knowledge represents only a minute fraction of our potential understanding. The full resources of our mental computer remain untouched. Humankind is still searching for the operating system with which to access those limitless reserves.

In this book, as well as through other tools and teachings of Kabbalah, you can at last gain possession of that system. Learning Kabbalah is like slipping a powerful application into the disk drive of the human computer. Of course, most of us do not learn to use a new program overnight. But little by little, we learn to accomplish our desired tasks and to avoid the pitfalls along the way. Rather than having to find a new solution to every problem we encounter, the kabbalistic frame of reference allows us to penetrate the root cause of each problem, thus averting the constant "crashes" life presents in the everyday world.

While the miraculous power of the human brain may remain forever beyond our understanding, we can gain a sense of our own inner workings through the careful application of kabbalistic principles. For we are models of creation — as it was, so it is, and so it will be. By understanding the microcosm of ourselves, we can connect with the macrocosm that is the infinite power of the universe.

Until recently, Kabbalah was a carefully hidden secret. But now the time has come to make Kabbalah available for all who have a desire to learn.

Read on . . .

Chapter I

ROOTS

The roots of Kabbalah extend deep into the soil of our primordial past. For most of humankind, those roots have been invisible. But certain individuals have always sought to establish links with a deeper reality. There have always been seekers for whom "face value" was never enough. There have always been those who looked for the word within the word, the thought within the thought, the meaning within the meaning.

When fools see a well-dressed person, they look no further. But thinking people know that the style of one's clothing has nothing to do with the body inside. Kabbalah teaches that the worth of the body lies in the soul. Just as the sheen and ripples on the surface of a pond hide what lies beneath, so does empirical existence obscure our true essence.

Confusion arises because there are two real worlds. One is the reality beyond change — complete, eternal, and infinite. The other is the so-called real world — a "reality" that changes with the tides, becoming larger and smaller, harder and softer, faster and slower, depending on how it is perceived. In the end, it is anything you want to make it. Hence, it is not "real" at all. The two realities of the lower and upper worlds are separated by only a hair's breadth — apart, yet together all the same. The kabbalist's task is to bridge the gap between these worlds — to see one within the other, and to see the universal, infinite soul in its finite, material expression.

To really comprehend the nature of the physical world, we must begin making connections with the metaphysical realm. To comprehend the nature of the external world, we must connect with the internal. Just because something is seen with the eyes does not mean it exists, any more than not seeing something is proof that it does not exist. Through Kabbalah, we peel away the layers of darkness in order to connect to the Light within.

Receiving

The literal meaning of the word Kabbalah is "receiving." The very fact that the secrets of the universe are revealed through the study of receiving tells us a great deal about the nature of existence. We learn that a desire to receive is the basic mechanism by which the world operates — the dynamic process at the basis of all physical and metaphysical manifestations.

This desire to receive affects all creation, whether human, animal, vegetable, or inanimate. In an inanimate object, of course, the desire to receive is minuscule. A stone needs nothing to ensure its presence. Nonetheless, for it to exist at all, it must contain some element of the desire to receive.

As we move up the hierarchy of creation, we find an increasing dependence on the external world for survival. This culminates in humankind, which of all creation has the greatest desire to receive. As men and women, we desire not only physical manifestations but also intangibles such as love, happiness, and fulfillment.

According to kabbalistic teachings, the culmination of the desire to receive is the desire to receive for others — that is, the desire to share. The desire to receive reaches completion only when it is transformed into the desire to share with the people around you.

Wisdom

In Hebrew, the word mysticism is rendered as *Chochmah haNistar*, the "wisdom of the hidden." But what is meant by "hidden"? Certainly, for most of us, the future is hidden — but to the extent that the future is revealed to us, we are wise. Thus, the sages of Kabbalah asked, "Who is wise?" And they answered, "Those who see the consequences of their actions."

A wise person's understanding penetrates to the root level. He or she does not have to wait for the future to transpire in order to see it clearly. With true wisdom, all subsequent happenings can be known. Kabbalah, then, may be understood as the acquisition of a wisdom that allows us to see the deepest meaning of creation in both the physical and metaphysical levels of our experience.

Armed with this wisdom, we can set out on a path that leads to fulfillment. Once we recognize what is truly real — once the veils of the material world have been stripped away — we can begin to achieve unity with creation, and with the Creator as well. What's more, we can begin to see that creation and Creator are one and the same.

Science

As the accomplishments of science have become more sophisticated, the workings of science have become less and less comprehensible. The further science progresses, the more its methods seem to lie beyond the grasp of the population as a whole, or even of scientists in other disciplines. The scientist-philosophers of earlier generations have given way to specialists who limit their fields of view in the hopes of being able to master some small corner of the physical world.

But because science restricts its investigations to the physical world, its findings are limited to the realm of effects. Science asks only how something exists within the dimensions or limitations of time, space, and motion. Kabbalah goes further and confronts the question of why things exist at all. It is the objective of Kabbalah to provide the bridges and connections between the physical world of "how" and the spiritual world of "why."

Kabbalah teaches that the fundamentals of physical science cannot be substantiated without reference to the spiritual dimension. Without the spiritual component, therefore, the objectives of science cannot be reached. This has been apparent even to scientists, although generally only to the greatest among them. As Stephen Hawking, the renowned astrophysicist, wrote in A Brief History of Time, "If we discover a complete theory . . . we shall all be able to take part in the discussion of the question of why it is that we and the universe exist. If we find the answer to that, it would be the ultimate triumph of human reason — for then we would know the mind of God."

Coincidence

We now come to another area of difference between science and Kabbalah — an area that in itself suggests why many people believe Kabbalah to be more complex and less accessible than science. This concerns the relationships between objects and events. When we can see no connection between two objects or events, we say they are unrelated. And if they suddenly seem to come into contact in an unexpected manner, we call this a coincidence. Yet the root of this word, coincide, denotes only that two events have occurred together. This serves to diminish and compartmentalize the event's significance. To the kabbalist, however, so-called coincidences are highly significant. They are windows through which we can see beyond the world of appearance and into the world of essence.

Language

The language of Kabbalah is the authentic human language; it permits us to appreciate its profound wisdom to the utmost extent of our capabilities. To a generation that has witnessed so many advances in complex areas of scientific research, the wisdom of Kabbalah can no longer be considered too remote or inaccessible. To the contrary, its most important teachings are becoming increasingly vital to the maintenance of stability and harmony in a confusing technological world.

Although Kabbalah often deals with profound matters, it does so in language that can be easily understood. This in itself is an important lesson. The method of disseminating knowledge in Kabbalah points to one of its central teachings: that the infinite world can be expressed even in the limited terminology of the physical world.

Symbols

To be sure, not all the concepts of Kabbalah are amenable to direct description. Analysis of the upper and lower worlds, for example, is often expressed through analogy and metaphor. Colorful images establish an imaginative link between the phenomena being described and the tangible world in which we live; were this not the case, the world described by Kabbalah would remain forever closed and inaccessible.

Through these images, we learn that the lower realm is patterned after the upper realm. As we read in the *Zohar* (the Book of Splendor), the basic text of Kabbalah, "Nor does the smallest blade of grass on the earth fail to have its specially appointed star in the heavens" (*Zohar I*, p. 34a).

All that exists in the upper world does, in time, reveal itself in a reflected image on earth — yet paradoxically, the totality of the upper and lower worlds always remains a single entity. This makes available the insight and knowledge required for our understanding of metaphysical concepts.

All of creation, for example — the upper and lower worlds — may be compared to a tree. It is the Kabbalistic Tree of Life, whose roots are buried deep beyond the reach of ordinary perception. But everything we see, hear, touch, or taste grows from those roots. Thus, through the principles of corresponding natures, we can observe the unknown upper realm by examining the interactions of that which lies below.

Just as electronic communications can be transmitted through cables, so too can we refer to prayers and precepts as cables. We use this imagery to emphasize their function as paths through which certain aspects of energy can be channeled. We are not, however, referring to the physical characteristics of a cable.

Secrets

The question of how we can be certain of the interpretation of the metaphysical plane revealed by the *Zohar* is carefully considered by its author, Rav Shimon bar Yochai: "And for those people who do not know, yet have a desire to understand," directs the *Zohar* (*Zohar III*, p. 99A), "reflect upon that which is revealed and made manifest (in this world), and you shall know that which is concealed inasmuch as everything (both above and below) is the same. For all that the Force has created in a corporeal way has been patterned after that which is above."

When Rav Shimon says, "When the angels descend, they clothe themselves in earthly garments" (*Zohar III*, p. 152a), he reveals two significant sodot (secrets): Spirituality, represented in the *Zohar* by the term angels, cannot reveal anything of its essence unless it is clothed in a corporeal garment. It is only when spirituality is thus clothed that outward actions and interactions reveal something of their essence. Human thought, before it is expressed as speech, remains hidden within the mind of the individual. This, then, is the first *sod* revealed by Rav Shimon: Metaphysical essence must be clothed in corporeal garments such as human speech, just as all actions and interactions that we observe are governed by metaphysical forces.

Now to the second secret in this passage of the *Zohar*: "Nor could the world bear to coexist with them if they were not thus clothed." To better understand this subtle but penetrating secret, consider electricity. We know that electrical current is an energy that must be contained within some sort of cable in order for it to be useful. In the case of a fallen power line or a broken cable, there is a danger of electric shock or fire. The flowing current is no longer contained, and anything it touches will be unable to hold this naked energy.

We also know that there is a potential for great danger when an imbalance exists between sharing positive forces and receiving negative forces. The overloading of an electrical cable signals trouble, since the receptacle or vessel lacks the insulation and safeguards for the controlled output of energy. In the metaphysical realm, the pattern is identical. The concepts of Kabbalah — the indelible truths — can be understood by those who read its language with their hearts and not just with their eyes, and who listen with their minds and not just their ears.

Conditions

Throughout history, those who knew and practiced Kabbalah took great care in disseminating that knowledge. Today's kabbalists know that it is not only proper but also necessary to make Kabbalah available to all who seek it.

Why was the *Zohar* concealed from earlier generations? It is not that they weren't ready for it. From a spiritual perspective, such generations were undoubtedly at a higher level of consciousness than our own and were thus better equipped to understand Kabbalah's profound wisdom. Discussions in the *Talmud* anticipate the questions being raised in this generation concerning the nature of spirituality and its change over time. In these discussions, the sages show that they are fully aware of the paradox at the center of the issue: The earlier generations, being more spiritual by nature, needed less in the way of spiritual knowledge from books, yet achieved more in the realm of working wonders and miracles. It appears that greater knowledge and more intensive study are less amply rewarded. The resolution of this paradox lies in the spiritual level achieved in different generations.

Earlier generations were, quite simply, closer to the source of spirituality than were later ones; they demanded and expected far less from the physical world. They were on a higher plane of existence. Being less dependent on the physical world, they could maintain their elevated status and exert control over the direction of the world through their spirituality. The expression of this control was the manifestation of "miracles" — the expression of their power over the natural order of the universe.

Later generations must rely to a larger extent on knowledge from secondary sources, such as the written word. At the same time, their greater dependence on the physical world — their desire to receive — also makes them more capable of receiving the Light. The receiving Vessels are of a coarser material, so to speak, but the Light, once it has penetrated, is present in a much more explicit form than in earlier generations.

Traditionally, the study of Kabbalah has been divided into two parts: secret teachings and basic principles. Secret teachings deal with mysteries on the subtlest level. And in dealing with the subtlest levels of manifest existence (such as the atom and its subatomic particles), there is danger. The secret teachings should therefore remain accessible only to those who have reached a point at which they can deal with the power contained therein. Consequently, this volume does not deal with secret teachings, focusing instead on basic principles.

As it is said, "When the student is ready, the teacher will appear." Yet the study of basic kabbalistic principles is not only possible but encouraged by the sages. Basic principles deal with the order and purpose of creation and lead to the very root of our existence and being. The traditional prohibitions against the study of the secret teachings should not be applied to the consideration of basic principles.

The prohibition against the study of basic principles was removed in the 16th century, when famed kabbalist Rav Abraham Azulai revealed a decree of the early sages. In the preface to his treatise entitled The Light of the Sun, Rav Azulai wrote, "From the year 1540 and onward, the basic levels of Kabbalah must be taught publicly to everyone young and old. Only through Kabbalah will we forever eliminate war, destruction, and man's inhumanity to his fellow man."

The Zohar itself also states that in our generation, even young children will understand Kabbalah and the inner truths of our world (Zohar III, p. 58a).

Chapter II

BEFORE THE BIG BANG

Know that before the emanations were emanated and the creations were created, the upper simple Light filled the entire existence and there was no empty space or vacuum whatsoever. For everything was filled with the Light of the Endless World.

Ten Luminous Emanations
Vol. 1, pp. 51–52

Like a dream that cannot quite be remembered, the Endless Light dances at the edge of our consciousness. And whether we know it or not, our subconscious minds are constantly striving to find that Light and to bring it into our awareness.

Most people are unaware that the Endless Light could be theirs, never comprehending the psychological and spiritual discomforts that Light could overcome or the inner needs it would so easily fulfill. Even the existence of a metaphysical world seems totally beyond their grasp. So they live their lives, unaware that their lack of attachment with the Light is the only reason for the desperation they experience every day. Through the teachings of Kabbalah, we discover the means by which to bring the Endless Light to our earthly table, so that we may partake of unearthly delights at every moment.

Creation began with the Thought of Creation — the intention of the Creator to share without limit or end. This thought was complete. Literally everything emerged from it.

In the same way, the more fully a thought is established in our own mind, the better the chance for a successful completion. Knowledge initiates the creative process, and complete knowledge brings it to completion.

The Phases of Existence

Phase 1: The Endless

There is nothing in all existence that is not included within the Endless.

> *Ten Luminous Emanations*
> Vol. 1, p. 105

Kabbalah teaches that the first state of existence is the *Ein Sof*, or Endless World — a spiritual dimension that lies beyond the immediate grasp of our senses. As its name implies, this state is without beginning or end and beyond the limits of time, space, or motion that exist in the physical world.

The *Ein Sof* is like a seed that contains all future manifestations in potential form but remains an unfragmented whole. Only when it begins to unfold do the many elements of the seed reveal themselves as separate entities: root, trunk, branch, and leaf.

In the 16th century, Rav Isaac Luria of Safed, also known as the Ari (lion) because of his powerful interpretations of Kabbalah, wrote that there were "no distinguishable or discernible levels or grades" at this stage of creation (Tree of Life, Gate 1, Branch II). When we speak of events taking place within the Endless, we should always bear in mind that these are merely distinctions we impose, not discrete operations within the Endless World.

Phase 1A: Intention

The entire existence was emanated and created by a single thought. This thought is the activator, the essence of the action, reward, and spiritual effort.

Ten Luminous Emanations

Inner Reflections, Ch. 1

All of Kabbalah derives from a single axiom: the Creator is all-inclusive and lacks nothing.

There is an immediate conclusion to be drawn from this statement. The Creator is good, since all evil stems from the same root, which is lack of fulfillment. We can see this in our own lives, in which all our jealousy, anger, and hatred are the result of frustrated desires.

Having said that the Creator is complete and therefore good, we can now describe the attribute of sharing through which we are made aware of the Creator's existence. This is the Creator's desire to share, which is described in Kabbalah as the Light.

We know from our life experiences that sharing is an attribute of goodness. If we consider any object or person whom we call good, we realize that the essential quality all good things share is their ability to give us something we desire. That something might be physical, emotional, intellectual, or spiritual.

The Light is sometimes called the "positive force" or "positive energy" because the Light is always complete and fills areas of incompleteness or negativity. The essence of this positive force is the desire to share.

The word desire is important here because it reminds us that there can be no sharing of something we do not possess. It might be thought that sharing, which is the only aspect through which the Creator is made known to us, implies that the source from which sharing emanates is diminished in the process. This, after all, is how things work in the material world: If we pour half a bottle of water into a glass, the bottle will contain less than before. The bottle is inanimate, and although it contains some small degree of a desire to receive (without which it could not exist), it does not have the power to draw down metaphysical energy for itself. When it shares, it is therefore diminished.

Can we then say that the Creator is diminished by sharing with us? To answer this question, think of a candle rather than a bottle. A candle's flame can light an infinite number of other candles without being diminished. To be sure, the candle itself will grow smaller the longer it burns, but this is merely the "body" or vehicle by which the light is transmitted; the light itself remains constant. This is because light does not belong to any of the four levels of existence — inanimate, vegetable, animal, or human. Like electricity, it is a natural force and a source of energy. As such, it has a close affinity to pure metaphysical energy, which gives us insight into the importance of Light in ritual and celebration.

The original Thought of Creation was the intention to share the Creator's boundless blessings. If we consider this experience of sharing in the material world, we realize that it assumes a certain desire on the part of the recipient. The mechanical act of transferring something from our possession to that of another person is in itself unsatisfactory. Clearly, there must be a desire to receive on the part of the recipient — knowledge of what the gift entails and signifies — before we can say we are truly giving. Provided that this desire is present, we may appear to have lost something in the act of giving, but our desire to receive is made far greater each time we share. Our apparent loss in the physical world is balanced by a gain in metaphysical power.

Phase 1B: Unity of Desire

From the force of the desire to share of the Emanator, the desire to receive was born inevitably in the emanated. This is the vessel in which the emanated receives the abundance.

> *Ten Luminous Emanations*
> Vol. 1

We have said that sharing is the Creator's defining attribute. We have also seen that there can be no sharing unless there is an entity that desires to receive. We should also note that the Creator's infinite desire to share includes a desire to fulfill every possible grade and quality of desire to receive; whether there was a desire for health, wisdom, money, or possessions, its fulfillment was contained in the original desire to impart. Although kabbalists speak of the receiving Vessel as if it were a single entity, we must remember that the Vessel is actually an infinite number of Vessels. Every one is the expression of a different desire, each receiving its individual fulfillment from the Creator.

The desire to receive is the first and basic form of every essential being.

> *Ten Luminous Emanations*
> Vol. 1

The creation of this Vessel, according to Kabbalah, was the beginning and the end of creation. All subsequent emanations and unfoldings are essentially no more than the multiplying results of the primal union of cause and effect, positive and negative, conduit and receiver.

The entire existence that is included in the *Ein Sof* is extended from an existence that already exists. Only the desire to receive is new.

> *Ten Luminous Emanations*
> Vol. 1

If all that existed was the desire to share, then all that was created was the desire to receive. The desire to share could not have been created itself, for the process of creation implies that something previously nonexistent has been brought into existence. Yet we have already stated that the essential characteristic of the desire to share lies in the fact that it is complete and lacks nothing. It is therefore inconceivable that the desire to share could be created, since, lacking nothing, existence must be one of its attributes.

We find this explained in Nachmanides' commentary in the line from the Morning Prayer: "He forms the light, and He creates the darkness." Nachmanides asks why two different words are used — formed and created — and concludes that the Light, the force of positive energy, could not be created. Creation indicates prior incompleteness, and the Light is always whole. Instead, it was formed — meaning that it was molded and circumscribed — so that it could descend from the Endless. However, it can be said that darkness had been created, since darkness is an indication of incompleteness and of the desire to receive. As such, it was not present in any form whatever within the Creator, but instead was created as a totally new phenomenon.

Phase 1C: Something from Nothing

All is drawn from a non-existing state.

> *Ten Luminous Emanations*
> Vol. 1

As a result of the Creator's original desire to share, which was the motivating factor behind creation, there arose the desire to receive, which is said to have sprung from "nothing." But nothingness should not be mistaken for emptiness. It is simply a state of preexistence, devoid of any attribute.

This idea is at once both simple and profound. All manifestations that unfold from this mystical nothingness are known in Kabbalah as the "hidden cause." Consequently, "nothing" is in fact immeasurably more real than any other form of existence. The whole world was made from it.

Phase 1D: Light and Vessel

A basic metaphor describing the process of giving and receiving involves the image of the Light as the sharing energy and the Vessel as the receiver. Kabbalah teaches that these are really different aspects of the same unified energy. They may be compared to the positive and negative poles of an electrical circuit, which are opposite in observable effect but are actually different manifestations of the same internal energy.

Phase 2: Arousal

The desire to receive is not completed in the emanated being, not until it is aroused from itself.

Ten Luminous Emanations
Vol. 1

A seed contains the potential for roots, leaves, branches, and blossoms. In the same way, the Endless includes both the Light and the Vessel — the desire to receive and the desire to share. But only after various conditions are met — moisture, soil, and sunlight — can the chain of events begin that will allow the undifferentiated elements within the seed to express themselves as separate entities.

If the Thought of Creation was to create a desire to receive, then the creation of the Vessel in its initial form in the Endless completely achieved this end. This Vessel is completely and everlastingly filled with Light and therefore cannot experience any desire to receive in itself. Indeed, its essence is indistinguishable from the Light, which is the desire to share.

A perfect balance thus existed between the endless giving of the Creator and the endless receiving of the creations. This equilibrium might have gone on forever had the desire to receive not aspired toward equality with the desire to share. With the arousal of a desire to share, the Vessel drew down an abundance of Light, known as the Light of Wisdom.

There now existed a situation in which the infinite number of Vessels all desired to share with one another. This is not possible, however, because at this stage each was completely fulfilled. At this phase, the Vessel emerged from a potential will to an actual will. The term phase should be understood in the sense of cause and effect, not in terms of time.

Phase 3: Withdrawal

. . . and the Light withdrew . . .

> *Ten Luminous Emanations*
> Vol. 1

The Vessels are so sensitive to one another's desire to share that each empties itself voluntarily of its Light. The vacuum caused by this withdrawal or shutting off is referred to as the third phase.

The Zohar likens this process to hewing a stone (*Zohar I*, p. 15a). At the moment the chisel strikes, an empty space is created in the stone. This is caused by the desire to receive's rejection of the Light from the desire to share. As a result of this emptiness, there is both a concealing of the Light of Wisdom and a concurrent sending forth of the Light of Mercy. Owing to the Vessel's desire for the Light of Mercy and not for the Light of Wisdom, revelation is still only potential with respect to the ultimate completion of the Vessel.

Phase 4: Completion

A commentary in the *Ten Luminous Emanations* (vol.

1, p. 6) reads, "This last grade in its complete perfection is found only in the *Ein Sof*, before the creation of all the worlds."

The lack of the Light of Wisdom, which is the undiminished Light, causes the Vessel to feel the loss of what it previously contained. As a result, it craves to receive the Light of Wisdom. Such craving establishes the full capacity of desire, bringing the Vessel to its completion as a receiving entity.

Let us return to the analogy of striking a stone. *The Zohar* (*Zohar I*, p. 15a) explains that the chisel's strike leaves an empty space in the stone, which causes a spark of friction. Like this spark, there is within the innermost recesses of the Endless a point known as the Central Point. It is the desire to receive with the capacity to hold the entirety of the Endless Light.

Kabbalists refer to the emergence of the Central Point as the Beginning — the source that led to all subsequent creations. This first word in the Book of Genesis, Bereshit "in the beginning", bears witness to the paramount importance of this instant, which is actually the final phase of the *Ein Sof*.

Here, then, for the first time, is the full paradigm for the existence of the desire to receive. The power of this desire again draws down the Light of Wisdom. This completes the establishment of the desire to receive and completes

the creation of the world of the Endless.
Impressions

Like echoes in a canyon, like muffled whispers in some
foreign tongue, like phrases that cannot quite be remembered, those nebulous impressions of our former unity
with the Endless Light haunt us — and sometimes even
irritate us. Unconsciously, unknowingly, these impressions link us with the supreme fulfillment that was ours
before the Big Bang, keeping us on our restless quest for
contentment.

Fulfillment is elusive. One can search for a lifetime and
never attain it. As rare and priceless as an artistic master-
piece, fulfillment is something most of us can appreciate
only from a distance. Like the Mona Lisa, it is not for sale
— but even if it were, it would lie far beyond our current
spiritual means.

Lasting fulfillment escapes most of us for a simple reason.
We each have but one true endeavor that can permanently fill and illuminate the seemingly vacant Vessel of
our being. At the Thought of Creation, this destiny was
revealed to all of us in the Endless. Our challenge is to
rediscover the single means by which we can reestablish
our affinity with the Light.

The real world is hidden from view by veils of negativity,
symptoms, and appearances. The revelation of the Endless Light within us can be accomplished in two ways.

One is trial and error, in which the seeker tries on new lifestyles, philosophies, diets, and spiritual doctrines as readily as a fashion model changes hats. Although not impossible, the likelihood of finding enduring fulfillment in this manner is rare. A far more effective approach requires an understanding of the process of mental, emotional, and spiritual evolution as taught by Kabbalah.

Through Kabbalah, we gain insights that allow us to trace our lives back to our primordial beginning in the *Ein Sof*, when we were truly One with the Light.

Chapter III

THE BIG BANG

In the beginning, before the universe became the multi-faceted environment in which we live today, a condition of mutual fulfillment existed between the Light and the Vessel. The endless sharing of the Creator was perfectly balanced with the endless receiving of His creations. The Creator gave endlessly of His beneficence, and the Vessel experienced satisfaction at endlessly receiving the Light. As we have discussed, this balanced condition might have gone on forever. But the Vessel, which incorporated all the human soul that would ever be created, felt ashamed at the one-sidedness of their relationship with the Creator. This condition, which results from receiving what is not earned, is referred to by the kabbalists as "Bread of Shame."

Bread of Shame

The natural consequence of eating unearned bread, of receiving something that is not earned by labor and endeavor, is embarrassment and shame! He eats the Bread of Shame.

Sefer Hakdamot, p. 52

A kabbalistic tale clearly illustrates this initially confusing concept. It recounts the story of a wealthy man who invited a number of friends to join him on some festive occasion. Just as the company was about to sit down to the meal, the host noticed a poor man passing by. He felt sorry for the man and instructed one of the servants to invite him in.

All the guests could see that the newcomer was badly in need of food and clothing. Yet when the host cordially invited the man to join them, they were astonished to hear him refuse. The host, bewildered by this unexpected reply, urged the poor man to reconsider. The poor man replied that he had no need for this sort of charity. The host insisted, the poor man politely refused — and so the conversation continued until the poor man finally relented. As he threw his hands in the air in a gesture of helplessness, he said, "Very well, if it really means that much to you, I'll accept your kind hospitality." With a sigh of relief, the guests sat down to begin the festivities.

In this story, the roles of donor and recipient are reversed, resulting in a heightening and sanctification of the transaction. To the poor man, receiving beneficence without having earned this kindness initially appears degrading. This is identical to the concept of Bread of Shame. What may be simple generosity on the part of the host takes on a new aspect in light of the poor man's inability to share anything in return. Generosity emerges as something unwanted — not because the poor man doesn't need food, but because there is no way (yet) that he can take it without losing his self-respect. Faced with the choice between humiliation and hunger, it is perhaps no longer surprising that he refuses the food.

Once this unexpected refusal of an obviously desired gift has taken place, however, the flow of energy in the situation begins to change. The rich man realizes that he has been deprived of an opportunity to do good. He insists, even pleads. He is no longer offering the poor man food, but asking him a favor!

Once the poor man sees how he can give as well as receive, he consents to join the feast. And so the rich man, too, both gives and gets. The cycle has been completed, with flow and feedback now in a state of dynamic balance.

We can apply this example to any form of benevolence. Unless there is a balance between donor and receiver, the original intention of the donor will not be realized. This holds true on all levels, beginning with the original Thought of Creation, which was to impart ineffable goodness to humanity.

A receiver who is not prepared to share, or one who is prevented from doing so, will inevitably reject the true intention of the donor. It was the Creator's wish and sole purpose to bestow abundance, but the Creator's creations could partake of this abundance only to the degree that their sense of shame would allow them. Therefore, the Creator complied and caused the desire to receive to withhold the Light so that it could redress the existing lack of balance.

Restriction

This withdrawal or contraction of the Light is known to kabbalists as the *Tsimtsum* (pronounced "zim-zum"), or restriction, whereby the Vessel greatly reduced its desire to receive the Endless Light. The Light itself did not cease to emanate its full benevolence to the Vessel and was not in any way affected by its restriction. Rather, the events of the restriction and the withdrawal of the Light concern only the reaction of the Vessel and its desire to receive.

The Endless World operates on the principle of cause and effect, with the sharing of the Light the cause and the receiving by the Vessel the effect. Inasmuch as the Light lacks nothing, the Vessel cannot impart anything to it. Thus, the only possible way for the Vessel to emulate the Light and become a cause is to reject the Light. With the ensuing process of restriction, the Vessel was catapulted (as were all of us) from the Endless World into the physical universe, which is governed by the laws of restriction.

For human souls, restricting the Light is the only way to receive its benefits. Through restriction, an unexpected result occurs. Rather than losing the Light, we make a place for it to be received consciously and with purpose — the purpose of sharing. The direct Light is too strong to be handled and would cause damage. In the presence of restriction, however, the mediated Light can safely fulfill the desire to receive.

The restriction imposed on humans is due to the nature of the soul, which is transformed on leaving its domain in the upper world so that it can live inside a body of flesh and blood. In the higher worlds, the soul experiences both the beneficence of the *Ein Sof* and the feeling of shame that results from the inability to impart anything to the Infinite. So the soul descends to this world to erase the feeling of shame — through restriction and by sharing with others who are also lacking.

Birth of the Universe

Following restriction, whereby the Light withdrew around the Central Point, there remained an empty space, atmosphere, or vacuum surrounding the Central Point.

> *Ten Luminous Emanations*
> Vol. 1, p. 65

The primordial restriction occurred in the Central or Primordial Point and caused a new state of being to appear. From this world, the Light was withdrawn and there was empty space — an expression of the unfulfilled desire to receive. The Central Point's emptiness was filled by time, space, and motion — the whole created universe, in all its variety and individuation.

This emptiness after restriction should be understood as the first effect. The surge of the Light into this emptiness was so overwhelming that it caused a shattering of the Vessel — which science calls the Big Bang. And since that time, no Light has been revealed in the created world without the Vessel. The Vessel limits the abundance of Light, accepting no more and receiving no less than what it desires to receive. There is no compulsion to receive the Light; everything depends on the motivating influence of the desire.

Desire

All that materialized after the Big Bang — every speck of matter and particle of cosmic dust — emerged with a need, a void that demands fulfillment. That void is the essence of all desire. And the need to fill the void that exists between the Creator and ourselves forms the basis of all psychological, physical, emotional, and spiritual yearnings.

Desire stems from an inner longing that has already attained and experienced its ultimate fulfillment. "It is impossible for any desire to be stirred up in existence unless at a previous time a fulfillment was revealed sufficient to that desire," the Ari teaches us. Desire in the upper worlds becomes necessity in the lower world.

Any physical effect is initiated by a cause on the metaphysical plane. Inasmuch as the Endless was the cause of everything, it encompassed every desire and every fulfillment that ever was or will be. We could not possibly long for anything of which we have no conception. A person born and raised in the rain forest, for example, is no more likely to suddenly develop an urgent craving for chocolate truffles than a Westerner is likely to be seized by a desire for live grubs. Cravings do not spring up of their own volition; the taste must have been tasted before.

Every desire we can ever have is already fulfilled in a potential state: Every sculpture has been sculpted, every building built, every wish already granted. Fulfillment precedes desire. The effect is already present within the cause.

Illusion

When the Light withdrew so that we could be absolved of Bread of Shame, emptiness and an illusion of darkness remained. It seemed that the Light had disappeared. Yet it is a keystone of kabbalistic thought that every manifestation, both physical and metaphysical, is imbued with the Light of Creation. How, then, can there be darkness?

In reality, the Light, which had formerly illuminated all phases of the Endless with equal magnitude, had been transformed and made manifest in a finite form. The

Light became obscured from our view as a result of negativity, which can accurately be described as a by-product of the desire to receive. This negativity, which the kabbalists refer to as husks or shells, encircles the Light like a curtain placed over a lamp. The Light is there in all its glory, but the viewer is unaware that it even exists. In a similar manner, metaphysical curtains cloud our perceptions and limit our spiritual potential.

In summary, there had been no unfulfilled desires prior to the Big Bang. But Bread of Shame was brought about by the inability of souls to earn the Light or to share their blessings with one another. The souls therefore caused restriction. And the resulting emptiness and absence of Light brought about the infinite desire to receive that permeates the physical world.

Our sensation of incompleteness and deficiency leads to chaos and disharmony. We are placed in this state so that we can eliminate Bread of Shame by restriction and by sharing — and in this way fulfill our own most fundamental desires.

Chapter IV

WORLDS BEYOND

"Why should we bother to know about them?"

Physicists inform us that we see but a fraction of what goes on around us. Even with the most powerful telescopes, we can see but a tiny portion of the universe — and conversely, even the strongest electron microscope reveals only a fraction of the atomic and subatomic realm. So when kabbalists tell us that most of what really goes on in this universe lies beyond the realm of finite understanding, they know well of what they speak. To accept the observable world as the totality of existence is to cheat ourselves of life's possibilities.

Rav Isaac Luria, the great 16th-century kabbalist, gave us a system with which to penetrate the crust of illusion that surrounds this physical world and to discover the infinite reality that exists beyond. With this system, we can become masters of our own destiny rather than slaves to deception. The Lurianic system reveals how we can participate in our own spiritual evolution, learning along the way to resist illusion and connect to metaphysical truth.

Before and After

Before the great restriction known to kabbalists as *Tsimt-sum*, we the emanated asked for and received the eternal and inalienable aspect of free will, which according to the kabbalist means that we could choose to reveal the Light or not reveal it. The Light that once filled our inner Vessels restricted and withdrew, but certain "impressions" or "residues" remained. And though we are unaware of it, these faint reverberations of our former unity with the Endless are the cause of our every move, maneuver, decision, and desire.

The Ari taught us that fulfillment is the cause of desire, not the other way around. Desire was born in the Endless, and to the Endless it yearns to return. Our Vessel will not be fulfilled until all the illumination it once contained shines with the same radiance as it did in the place without end.

Having pondered this wisdom in great depth, the Ari advanced a concept that is so elegant in its simplicity that all phases of life and all aspects of existence fall under it. The concept involves only two stages or conditions. The first stage consists of desire that is fulfilled, as epitomized by the universal condition before restriction. The second stage includes desire that is unfulfilled, as exemplified by all that happened after restriction.

By thus defining the scope of existence, the Ari arrived at a formula for every conceivable area of life or situation. All of humanity's trials and tribulations — all of life and growth, and every thought, word, deed, and physical manifestation — can be explained and understood according to its stage of fulfilled or unfulfilled desire. Desire is constantly seeking fulfillment, just as Light is endlessly available to fulfill.

From this perspective, there would appear to be only one question that is truly worth asking: "Am I in a state of fulfilled or unfulfilled desire?" Or, put another way, "Am I revealing the Light or concealing it?"

Worlds

A kabbalist seeks to return to the seed level of his existence. The seed contains, in potential form, all the attributes of the four phases that have yet to be manifest. By looking at the seed, the kabbalist can see the past, present, and future — the beginning, the middle, and the end. With each subsequent phase, the vision or perspective becomes less apparent. The view is not as clear from the perspective of the second phase as from that of the first, and it gets dimmer still as we enter this world, where the Endless Light is completely obscured by negativity.

Kabbalah is a multilayered study. When we discuss the creation of the world, we are also speaking of the emergence of self-awareness. Through our understanding and conscious reenactment of the process of creation, we begin to unravel, connect, and illuminate our inner selves.

The process that took place after the Big Bang resulted in the emanation of five dimensions, or *Sefirot*, which mirror the phases of the Endless.

1. The Primordial Man

The *Sefirah* (singular of *Sefirot*) of *Keter*, or crown, forms the prototype of humankind, from which the soul of humanity derives its highest level of consciousness. From a cosmological standpoint, this stage was the interval immediately following the Big Bang, when Light and Vessel, energy and matter, were still intimately connected by similarity of form. The universal condition existing at this time so closely resembled the state in the Upper Light, where Light and Vessel were fused, that any distinction between them was almost imperceptible. Only later did the Light withdraw, with the universe developing into its present divided form.

2. The World of Emanation

This is the world of the *Sefirah* of *Chochmah*, or wisdom, and is the completion of the first phase of the Light's emanation. It has no consciousness in and of itself, as its only aspiration is to extend the Light to all phases of creation. *Chochmah* can be likened to the roots of a tree. In the words of the Ari, "From it is drawn all forms of wisdom found in the world."

3. The World of Creation

This second phase in the process of creation is the *Sefirah* of *Binah* — intelligence or understanding. Although this phase represents a significant lessening of the original Light of Wisdom, it is considered the ultimate state of metaphysical awareness any person can hope to achieve in the material world.

4. The World of Formation

The World of Formation is the *Sefirah* of *Zeir Anpin*, often referred to as the Small Face. This can be compared to the moon's reflection of the sun. The moon is a metaphor for the Small Face, while the sun is a metaphor for Long Face, or *Chochmah*, the first "extension" of the Light. From the phase of the World of Formation, each person receives his or her spiritual essence.

5. The World of Action

This fourth phase, the *Sefirah* of *Malchut*, or kingdom, is our physical world, and the only realm in which the revelation of the purpose of creation takes place. It is from this world that the lowest level of consciousness is extended to humankind. In the plant kingdom, the fruit represents the fourth phase. The other phases evolve automatically, without the necessity of an action — but now we must exert effort and labor in order to reveal Light. This condition was our choice in our efforts to remove Bread of Shame. Therefore, it is a kabbalistic principle that the revelation of Light can occur only within the fourth phase, or the lowest level — so those who reside here are responsible for manifesting the Light of Creation.

Nothing exists in this observable world that has not gone through the four phases of creation: not thoughts, words, deeds, growth, movement, or relationships; neither the manufacture nor the evolution of physical objects. Even our very lives become manifest only after the four phases have concluded. According to Kabbalah, each person proceeds through four distinct yet interconnected evolutionary phases in order to complete the cycle of his or her existence. Of all the creatures on this planet, only humans have the ability to bring this process to a conscious level and, having done so, to adapt it for use as a means of attaining cosmic awareness and personal awakening.

Bottled-up Energy

When a baby is born, the doctor or midwife counts its toes and fingers. If the total in each case is ten, the child is declared "perfect." On a much larger scale, mathematics — our most perfect system in the sense of being most absolute — is also based on the foundation of ten. From hit parades to movies and restaurants reviews, it seems that almost everything in this physical realm of existence is measured on a scale of one to ten. Ten is also a key number in the metaphysical realm.

Every aspect of life — every manifestation, physical or metaphysical — must advance through four phases. Each of these phases includes ten stages, or the ten *Sefirot* often referred to as Luminous Emanations. Whether we are speaking of earth, water, or air, all the stars and planets, or every speck of cosmic dust in the universe, all are composed of the ten attributes, or *Sefirot* — each of which is in turn composed of infinite permutations of ten within ten within ten.

The *Sefirot* or Vessels form the system used in Kabbalah to describe the process by which the unified energy of the Endless is refracted from the upper world to the lower levels. The *Sefirot* in the World of Restriction are patterned after their counterpart Vessels in the Endless World. Each *Sefirah* represents a different aspect of energy. Every complete structure that is manifested in the universe contains the ten *Sefirot*.

The emanation of a complete structure is called a countenance. In it will always be found the five *Sefirot* or levels of emanation known as *Keter* (crown), *Chochmah* (wisdom), *Binah* (intelligence), *Zeir Anpin* (Small Face), and *Malchut* (kingdom). The *Sefirah Zeir Anpin* is actually six *Sefirot*: *Chesed* (mercy), *Gvurah* (judgment), *Tiferet* (beauty), *Netzach* (victory), *Hod* (majesty), and *Yesod* (foundation). The total is ten.

These ten *Sefirot*, or energy-intelligences, are depicted in a system of columns referred to as the Tree of Life. The *Sefirot* in the Right Column reflect the characteristic of sharing and are described as positive. The *Sefirot* in the Left Column have the characteristic of receiving and are referred to as negative. The *Sefirot* in the Central Column represent balance, keeping the energy of the Right and Left Columns in check. Each *Sefirah* has all the characteristics, but one is dominant. The following is a brief description of each.

Keter (Crown)

The seed of each level is called *Keter*, derived from the word crowning or surrounding, because *Keter* is said to surround the entire "face" or countenance from above.

Keter is the purest of all levels, but it is also the most ambiguous. From our limited perspective, *Keter* appears to change its nature from Light to Vessel and back again, depending on the point of view. Like an optical illusion, *Keter* is one thing and then another — and while mentally we can grasp the idea that it is two things at once, we are incapable, from our finite perspective, of encompassing both "realities" at the same time.

When a king wears a crown, he is recognized as royalty — but without it, when he walks among the "people" in common clothes, there is no way to distinguish him from any one of his subjects. By virtue of its ambiguity, *Keter* seems uncertain whether it is in its original domain or part of the next level.

Chochmah (Wisdom)

Chochmah, or wisdom, is a Vessel of such a pure quality that its essence is transparent, lying beyond our perceptions. *Chochmah*, like *Keter*, defies finite understanding — and so again, as with *Keter*, its cause is interpreted according to what we can ascertain by studying its effects.

"Who is wise? He who sees what is born." This ancient saying speaks of the quality of wisdom. From the Lurianic perspective, this means that a wise person has the ability to look at any situation and see all of its potential consequences — all of its phases, possible outcomes, and manifestations. Rav Ashlag, the author of a commentary on the *Zohar* and one of the greatest kabbalists of the 20th century — my teacher's teacher — describes someone who has achieved a level of wisdom as follows: "He sees all future consequences of the thing observed, to the very last one." Rav Ashlag continues: "Every definition of complete wisdom is simply a form of seeing what is born, from each and every detail of existence, right to the last result."

Unlike *Keter,* of which we have no direct reference, *Chochmah* permits us some firsthand or direct experience. Sudden inspirations, flashes of intuition — these glimpses into our own unique fulfillment are the blessing of *Chochmah.* They are considered gifts, coming only to those who merit them.

Binah (Intelligence)

The nature of *Binah* is the awakening in the Vessel of the desire to share. This is the first conscious activity on the part of the Vessel, and that consciousness itself is the root cause for the manifestation of a new transformation of Light. *Binah* represents a form of self-awareness that does not exist in preceding *Sefirot.* And it is through her awareness of her own being as well as her desire to share that *Binah* transforms the Light of Wisdom into a light of a wholly different and "inferior" expression, the Light of Mercy. Each exertion on the part of the Vessel creates a denser atmosphere around the Light, and thus the Light found within each level of Vessel is said to be "inferior" to that of the Vessel before. "Inferior" refers here not to the quality of the Light itself, which is flawless, but to the degree of Light that each Vessel is capable of revealing.

Potential Connections

The *Sefirot* of *Keter, Chochmah,* and *Binah* together are known as the Head, or the First Three. They pave the way for both the physical and metaphysical emanations by connecting with the potential of each new phase. They are grouped together because they operate beyond the realm of everyday consciousness and precede the observable phases of physical manifestation. Having great affinity with the Light and little similarity with the World of Restriction, the First Three exist in an almost totally pure state — remaining, like the inner operation of a seed, invisible to the naked eye and beyond the realm of everyday consciousness.

The First Three play a vital behind-the-scenes role in every thought and physical manifestation. Although they are present only in the potential state, they must still be considered a part of every creative process. The beauty of potential is that it has affinity with potential everywhere. Potential is not a part of the World of Restriction, but rather an attribute of the Endless. All of us can connect with the potential in any dimension, and the act of connecting potentialities is the first step in any thought, growth, or physical manifestation.

The First Three can be likened to the point of a pencil. Before a person picks up a pencil, the First Three must have made a connection with the metaphysical (thought) level as well as with the end result of whatever a person hopes to manifest. A subconscious activity has taken place in which the completed image or text has already, in some sense, been completed in the person's mind. The moment the tip of the pencil touches the paper, a new phase begins: that of the physical process.

Zeir Anpin (Small Face)

The first three *Sefirot* — *Keter*, *Chochmah*, and *Binah* — are the means by which Light enters this world. They do not affect our physical world other than directing Light into it. *Zeir Anpin*, or Small Face, represents the gathering or funneling of the forces of the universe in preparation for the tidal wave of revelation that will take place in *Malchut*, the final *Sefirah*.

Small Face comprises two triads of emanations: *Chesed*, *Gvurah*, and *Tiferet*; and *Netzach*, *Hod*, and *Yesod*. Together with the final *Sefirah* of *Malchut*, these *Sefirot* are the channels of energy by which the universe becomes physically manifested. kabbalists understand these seven *Sefirot* through the biblical personalities known as the "chariots." They are the vehicles or conduits by which these particular cosmic energies were "drawn down" from their potential state in the metaphysical realm to an active form in our universe.

Chesed (Mercy)

The energy of *Chesed* — mercy or kindness — comes from the Right Column, which represents the desire to share. The patriarch who drew down this energy was Abraham. We know that Abraham was always ready to welcome guests into his home; the Talmud explains that this is the reason his house had four doors. Abraham's capacity for giving was so vast that even after his circumcision, when he was suffering greatly, he went out to look for people with whom he could share. 'So the Creator caused a period of unusually hot weather, so that people would stay at home instead of disturbing Abraham's rest and recovery' (Genesis 18:1).

Gvurah (Judgment)

The second of the seven *Sefirot* is *Gvurah*, expressing judgment or strength. It is symbolized by the biblical personality of Isaac. The energy of *Gvurah* is part of the Left Column, because it is associated with the desire to receive. In the Torah portion on the binding of Isaac, it becomes evident how the Left Column (Isaac) is tempered or bound by the Right Column (Abraham), preparing the way for the emergence of the Central Column (Jacob). Jacob is the essential balancing factor that enables the Right Column to use the energy of the Left Column without destroying it entirely. *Gvurah* is the force of judgment, not in the sense of punishment, but rather in the sense of the inevitable repercussions that occur when the desire to receive is exercised without first removing Bread of Shame. Therefore, when we read that "Isaac loved Esau because he did eat of his venison" (Genesis 25:28), Esau represents the desire to receive for the body alone, without any desire to give. Isaac was the means by which that selfish desire was transformed into a Desire to Receive for the Sake of Sharing.

Tiferet (Beauty)

Jacob represents the Central Column, the *Sefirah* of *Tiferet*, or beauty — as indicated by the verse "And Esau was a cunning hunter, a man of the fields, but Jacob was a quiet man, dwelling in tents" (Genesis 25:27). The word for quiet used in the Torah also means complete, indicating that with Jacob the three-column system of Left, Right, and Central Columns was complete. *Tiferet* is also used as another name for the entire group of the six *Sefirot* of *Zeir Anpin*, indicating its added importance. The existence of the Central Column is the aspect associated with the children of Israel. It is therefore fitting that Jacob, who is also called Israel (Genesis 32:29), should be the father of the 12 tribes of Israel. These 12, in turn, represent the 12 signs of the zodiac that influence our world — a further example of the totality that we associate with Jacob.

Netzach (Victory)

The fourth chariot is Moses, who represents the *Sefirah* of *Netzach*, victory or endurance — the energy of the Right Column. In the battle between the Israelites and Amalek, Moses stood on a hill and controlled the course of the battle by raising or lowering his hands (Exodus 17:11). Moses was given the honor of receiving the Torah on Mount Sinai because it was through his strenuous effort that he achieved total understanding.

Hod (Majesty)

The *Sefirah* of *Hod* (majesty) is represented by Aaron, who belonged to the tribe of Levites. The energy of *Hod* is the manifestation of the total energy of the Left Column in this world (*Zohar III*, p. 151b), indicated by the splendor of Aaron's robes when he became Cohen Gadol (high priest). It should be noted, however, that the role of Cohen belongs to the Right Column, representing the energy-intelligence of sharing. This is a result of Aaron's achievement: transforming his nature of judgment into one of loving kindness.

Yesod (Foundation)

Joseph, the son of Jacob, is also a chariot of the Central Column. Therefore it is written, "Israel loved Joseph" (Genesis 37:3), indicating a similarity of spiritual energy. Joseph represents the *Sefirah* of *Yesod*, or foundation. Through him, all the energy of the upper *Sefirot* of *Zeir Anpin* is funneled down to the physical level. Joseph is the storekeeper who dispenses spiritual nourishment to the people. In the same way, he was chosen by Pharaoh to control the sorting and distribution of food in the years of plenty and famine in Egypt (Genesis 41:56; *Zohar I*, p. 197a).

Malchut (Kingdom)

King David represents the last *Sefirah*, which is *Malchut*, or kingdom. *Malchut* is the desire to receive, as well as the world in which we live. King David was a man of war and conflict, epitomizing the struggle for existence on this physical level. Because of his warlike nature, he was considered unworthy to build the Temple. More than any of the other chariots, he represents the battle of good and evil associated with the "kingdom" of this world (*Zohar Hadash*, p. 67c). *Malchut* reveals the purpose of creation: transforming potential to actual, exposing the hidden, and materializing the immaterial. It also awakens the desire to receive for oneself alone. This powerful force of attraction, the negative aspect of desire, is likened to gravity. It is the earth's primal motivating energy-intelligence, which, when translated into human nature, is greed. Because it possesses more desire to receive than all the other Vessels combined, however, it is capable of the greatest revelation of Light.

This brief exposition on the nature of the *Sefirot* and their connections with the chariots should provide new insights into the stories of the Torah. When studying them, bear in mind the characteristics of each *Sefirah* and attempt to understand events in terms of the "bottled-up energy" that each event represents.

Curtains

There are two modes of restriction. The first is voluntary, and the second, known as the Curtain, is involuntary. Either we choose to restrict our desire to receive for ourselves alone, or the restriction will occur through the activation of the Curtain. This is a consequence of our own making. The *Tsimtsum* resulted from our desire to be released from the burden of Bread of Shame. As a result of that initial restriction, we can no longer receive anything in good conscience that has not been earned.

Unlike the *Tsimtsum*, which is totally resolute, the Curtain represents a flexible form of restriction. Like a window curtain, it allows more or less light in according to the degree of resistance with which it is confronted. A small gust of wind, for example, will create only a small opening in the curtain, whereas a larger gust will create a larger opening, and a hand can push back the curtain completely, allowing light to stream into the room unobstructed. In a similar manner, the curtains of negativity that surround everything in this fourth phase, *Malchut*, can be opened through restriction, an act of will.

Compulsive behavior of any kind is an indication of desire to receive for oneself alone, whether one is compulsive about food, alcohol, cigarettes, drugs, work, or sex. All compulsive behaviors have the potential to provoke one of two kinds of restriction: Either the smoker voluntarily restricts her intake of smoke (restriction), or emphysema or some other involuntary ailment (curtain) will do it for her. The overeater can consciously restrain his appetite (restriction), or high blood pressure or cholesterol will create a life-threatening situation (curtain). Either the alcoholic stops drinking, or her liver gives out. The workaholic consciously restricts his hours, or a heart attack does it for him. If individuals do not learn to consciously restrict the indulgence of that to which they are addicted, it will be — forgive the old adage — "curtains" for them.

Returning Light

The Ari, Rav Isaac Luria, classifies Light according to two divisions: Straight Light and Returning Light. From the human perspective, the latter is by far the more important. Straight Light becomes manifested only upon contact with resistance. Sunlight, the physical equivalent of Straight Light, is revealed only when it reflects off something physical. This reflected light is call Returning Light by the kabbalists. It is Returning Light that is indisputably of greater importance as far as we of *Malchut* are concerned — for the simple reason that Returning Light is the only light that is revealed and thus the only light we ever see.

Line and Circle

Desire has two faces: the Desire to Receive for the Purpose of Sharing, an attribute of the circle, and the Desire to Receive for Oneself Alone, a characteristic of the line. Desire is humanity's most critical asset in the struggle for physical survival, but it is also our greatest obstacle on the path toward personal and planetary redemption. It is our most negative trait but at the same time affords our greatest opportunity for correction. By restricting the negative aspect of desire, we create a circular concept, an affinity or similarity of form between the Light and the Vessel — thereby converting the negative aspect of desire into the positive aspect of desire.

For the kabbalist, the sphere and the circle are symbols rich in meaning. The sphere is an example of perfect symmetry; it remains the same regardless of the angle from which it is viewed. The circle, a one-dimensional representation of the sphere, symbolizes infinity. Having no beginning and no end, it stands for the unity and perfection that was the domain of the Endless World before the withdrawal and restriction.

The line, on the other hand, is made up of a beginning, a middle, and an end. While the circle represents infinity, the line serves to illuminate that which is finite. Whereas the universal condition that existed before the restriction is described as being circular, the condition after the restriction formed a finite, linear dimension, represented by the line.

The line is represented by the biblical character of Adam. Both represent the first limitation. After the "fall" of

Adam, the souls of human beings became linear, or finite.
No longer were the souls of humans an unexpressed
aspect of the endless wheel of creation. The pure spirit
that was human moved into a body that was finite, with a
beginning, a middle, and an end.

Vessel Categories

Kabbalah classifies the *Sefirot* into two categories: the
encircling *Sefirot* and the *Sefirot* of straightness. Before
restriction, the circular Vessels were eternally satiated
with the Light of Creation. Restriction, however, created a condition in which the Infinite Light contained
within the encircling *Sefirot* would remain concealed
until activated by the *Sefirot* of straightness. The circular
Sefirot originated within the Endless, whereas the *Sefirot*
of straightness were an outgrowth of the subsequent
limited creative process — the line. The encircling *Sefirot*
are considered superior by virtue of their proximity to
the Endless.

The Encircling Vessels cannot and must not receive illumination in the infinite sense; otherwise, all desire would
be inundated by the omnipotent Light of the Endless.
In that event, the original purpose of creation would
be defeated; the Light would engulf the Vessel, and the
universe would revert to its original condition with the
undifferentiated energy-intelligence, receiving endlessly
of the Light's beneficence. The Vessel would again experience a sense of dissatisfaction at having no way to absolve

Bread of Shame.

The encircling *Sefirot* provide the impetus for all activity in the World of Restriction. They initiate all of our unconscious yearnings to return to our original infinite condition. Were it not for these primal memories of past fulfillment, we would be devoid of all longing and desire.

We of *Malchut* can find no peace until the Light contained within the encircling *Sefirot* has been restored to its former brilliance. But in this phase of existence, that possibility is remote. The finite nature of the *Sefirot* of straightness precludes the possibility of filling our Encircling Vessels to their fullest capacity.

True and lasting fulfillment can still be attained in this the World of Restriction, but infinite perfection cannot. According to the ancient texts, the complete illumination of all the Encircling Vessels will occur only when the corrective process has come full circle.

The Vessels of the ten *Sefirot* of straightness are called pipes because they limit and control with great precision the Light drawn through them. Just as the capacity of a pipe is gauged by its diameter and by the volume of water that can flow through it, so too is the capacity of the *Sefirot* of straightness measured in exact proportion to the Vessel's degree of longing.

Creative Process

Let us now describe the method by which the Light descends through the four phases — the creative process. The head of the line enters the circle of *Keter*. The Light strikes the Curtain, and much of the Light is repelled. The resistant action of the Curtain allows the First Three of the line to illuminate all ten *Sefirot* of *Keter* of the circles.

Only the First Three of the *Sefirot* of straightness (line) — *Keter*, *Chochmah*, and *Binah* — can meld and be encircled by the ten *Sefirot* of *Keter* of the circular Vessels (circle). The First Three, you will remember, exist in a nonobservable state of potential. Like attracts like. Hence, the affinities in the First Three of the line can connect with the affinities of the ten circular Vessels. This blending of similarities is the first of many stages in which the finite and the Infinite unite for the sake of mutual revelation.

The Curtain also allows a lesser amount of Light (Returning Light) to be drawn downward. The diffused Light descends, passing through the lower seven straight *Sefirot* of crown and down through the First Three of the next phase, *Chochmah*, where it strikes the Curtain of that phase and the process is repeated.

Just as the energy of the seed must first establish itself as a root before a trunk can come into being, and the trunk before the branch, and the branch before the leaf, so must the Light travel through the lower seven of each phase before it can illuminate the adjacent level below. The Light, in other words, must pass through the lower seven straight *Sefirot* of *Keter* before *Chochmah*'s Light of Wisdom can manifest. It must then pass through the lower seven of *Chochmah* before *Binah*'s Light of Mercy can be revealed. The same process is maintained throughout the ten levels of all four phases.

Light descends through one layer to the next, becoming more and more concealed until, by the time it arrives at this lowest level, *Malchut*, it is almost totally devoid of illumination. The Ari was most meticulous in his explanation of the process by which the Curtain, through involuntary resistance, allows all of the three previous phases — including *Malchut*, the phase of revelation of the Light — to become animated, and how we, the emanated, can attain contentment only through conscious restriction. It is at the last phase that the repelling of Light is referred to as the Curtain of *Malchut*.

While one level of consciousness may be higher than the next, in essence they are all identical. The only difference between *Chochmah*, the highest phase, and *Malchut*, the lowest, lies in the degree of concealment of Light. *Chochmah* is least concealed and *Malchut* most concealed — but in truth, both consist of the same Light.

The Ari explained this using the analogy of a lantern covered by layer after layer of thin fabric veils. Each layer or veil conceals the light further. Consider a situation in which one person enters a room at the moment another is placing the last of 100 veils. The light still seems as bright as ever. The new observer, who sees no lantern, quite naturally but mistakenly concludes that the first person has before him nothing more than a pile of cloth. Such is the prevailing condition here in *Malchut* as it relates to the Light. In *Malchut*, we have the paradox of Straight Light being most concealed as well as the possibility of Returning Light being most revealed through restriction.

The restriction of the Light and the ensuing Big Bang created the world of fragmentation in which we find ourselves. As a result of that moment, we must continually reestablish the connection with the Light through the limited creative process called the line.

Step by Step

We can now begin to study some of the esoteric kabbalistic text written by the Ari. A detailed analysis of even a single sentence of the Ari's writings could fill a chapter in and of itself — but my intention here is to provide readers with enough of an overview to initiate further study. Read the following detailed (though greatly simplified) interpretations with a certain degree of caution, keeping in mind that the real connection to this material cannot be gained merely through the intellect.

The Ari stated that "light which emerges according to the laws of the four phases, step by step, from pure to thick or impure, then stops at the fourth phase, is called Straight Line."

The first phrase of the sentence reads, "Light which emerges according to the laws of the four phases." What does this mean? The word light, as used here, refers to the four stages of the desire to receive through which all physical manifestations must proceed in their evolution. They are (1) Emanation (wisdom); (2) Creation (intelligence); (3) Formation (Small Face), which is further subdivided into Mercy, Judgment, Beauty, Endurance, Majesty, and Foundation; and (4) Action (Kingdom) or *Malchut*, which is this world of physicality.

As we learned earlier, the line is a convenient means by which to conceptualize the finite. In other words, before the restriction, the Light of the Endless was infinite and was hence deemed circular, while later, after the restriction, the Light took on a finite quality designated as linear (hence the concept of the line).

The descent of the Upper Light to the impure Vessels of the fourth phase is described as being straight because just as the earth's gravity exerts a direct influence on a falling stone, so too do the Vessels of straightness, whose longing is strong, cause light to descend "swiftly in a

Straight Line." Straight illumination is direct and finite.
Circular illumination is infinite.

Let us now examine another of the Ari's observations on
the extension of Light into the void:

"When the Light of the Endless was drawn in the form of
a Straight Line, the void, it was not drawn and extended
immediately downward. Indeed it extended slowly — at
first, the Line of Light began to extend and at the very
start of its extension in the secret of the Line, it was
drawn and shaped into a wheel."

Here again, the language can be confusing. Words like
immediately and slowly refer to time, but as we know,
spiritual time has nothing to do with chronological time.
Immediately, in this instance, means "without a change
of degrees." In other words, the Light of the Endless was
changed very little in the first stage of emanation, which
is known as Primordial Man. The word slowly, on the
other hand, means "evolution of degrees," referring to
the four phases — Emanation, Formation, Creation, and
Action — that are necessary for existence on a physical
level. When the Ari speaks of Light being "drawn" in a
straight line, it is possible that the image of a pencil or
other writing implement might enter the reader's mind.
Clearly, however, the Ari was not speaking of drawing a
line. Rather, the word drawn, as used here, is similar to
the connotation of that word as it is used in the phrase

"drawing water from a well." Desire draws the Light through its phases.

The final segment of the sentence reads, "The Line of Light began to extend, and at the very start of its extension in the secret of the Line, it was drawn and shaped into a wheel." The word wheel refers here to a *Sefirah* of circles, meaning that very little had changed in the first phase of Emanation, Primordial Man. The Light still had a connection with the Infinite. Circular Light reveals no gradations, no "above and below." The four grades of desire to receive were present in the world of Primordial Man (as they were in the Endless before the restriction), but they were not yet individuated. Hence, the Light of the line is said to have been "dressed in the circle."

The Circular Concept

Some people are connected with the Endless Light, while others are not. The difference is affinity. Those who wish to live in a circular context with the Endless may do so by creating an affinity with the Light. Affinity is a circular concept. The Light cannot reveal the Encircling Vessels, which are the essence of humanity and the universe, unless the Vessel desires revelation.

Through the limited creative process of the line, we can reveal the Endless Light that surrounds us. At the same time, we can awaken the Endless Light of the Encircling Vessels within. The circle can connect with the line only when and if the line makes the connection. We are the line, and only we can link our Inner Light with the circle of the Endless. Through desire to share, we create affinity; and through affinity, we reveal the Light.

Desire to receive, as the reader is by now well aware, has two aspects: one is to share, and the other is to receive for oneself alone. People possessed by the latter can never know the Light. The Curtain of their negativity repels the Light they may attract. Conversely, those who seek Light for the sake of sharing create an affinity with the Light by living within a circular context, and can therefore draw Light in direct accordance with their needs.

Chapter V

QUEST FOR BALANCE

An understanding of the nature of balance is essential to a proper understanding of Kabbalah. In fact, it might be said that to comprehend balance is to comprehend the very workings of nature itself. Everything strives toward balance. Negative seeks positive; cause seeks effect; darkness seeks light. The Light, which is the desire to impart, seeks the Vessel, or the desire to receive.

From a kabbalistic point of view, in the spirit-body spectrum, energy or spirit is connected with the Light or life-giving entity, while the body is the material expression of the energy that results from a melding of the two.

Everything in the physical world was and is endowed in varying degrees with both Light and Vessel attributes. The following chart describes how the principle of Light and Vessel apply to our world.

LIGHT	VESSEL
Desire to Share	Desire to Receive
Light	Dark
Male	Female
Positive	Negative
Sender	Receiver
Proton	Electron
Plus	Minus
Intellect	Intuition
White/reflective	Black/absorbent
Alkaline	Acidic
Hard	Soft
Active — doing	Passive — being
Perfection	Completeness
Proaction	Reaction

Energy Flow

Before the Big Bang, Bread of Shame caused the Vessel to deny the endless flow of Light or Energy, and this denial brought about the restriction that granted a degree of free will to the Vessel. Henceforth, it became the universal condition that the Light would flow according to the instructions given to it by the Vessel. From that moment on, it became our responsibility to control the input valves of our own creation.

If the inward flow is too great, the pipe is apt to burst; if it is too scant, the pipe may become too corroded to allow any energy to pass through it. An even flow of energy is essential to a person's physical, emotional, and spiritual well-being.

Just as children sometimes attempt to hide from their playmates by covering their eyes with their hands, so does the negative person hide from the Light of Creation. And just as children who grow weary of the darkness peek through the cracks between their fingers, so too can negative people, in a manner of speaking, open the fingers of their beings and see the Light — the magnitude of which will be directly proportional to the size of the opening.

There is no coercion in spirituality. The Light demands nothing from the Vessel. The Vessel's own desire is the sole determining factor in the manifestation of the Light.

Earth has a tremendous desire to receive (gravity), which it exerts in an endless effort to draw to itself anything and everything within the wide radius of its field of influence. Earth and all of its creatures, with the single exception of humans, have an inborn restricting mechanism that seeks to balance cause with effect, compelling them to take only according to their specific needs and to give equal measure in return. Having no built-in restrictive mechanism, humans are easy prey to a debilitating malady peculiar only to them: the desire to receive for the self alone, which might be loosely defined as greed.

Achievement

Why do some people soar like eagles while others must
burrow like moles? Why do some seem to drive straight
to their destinations while others meet with an endless
variety of roadblocks and detours? Why is it that some
seem destined to accept a lowly fate while others come
much closer to reaching their full potential?

Kabbalah teaches that while some of the desire we possess is determined by past incarnations, some degree of
longing — sufficient to meet our spiritual needs — is
inborn desire that does not change throughout each
lifetime. Desire creates movement. People who are born
with a greater degree of desire have more spiritual ground
to make up, so to speak, and therefore feel compelled to
accomplish more than others. Certain individuals who
are born with strong desires, for example, may fail to
achieve their full potential, while others who are born
with comparatively little desire prosper emotionally,
spiritually, and financially. The reason for this discrep-
ancy lies in the ability of the person with the lesser desire
to transform the desire to receive for the self alone into
the desire to share.

In more personal terms, people who have a great degree
of desire to share will receive the Light in direct proportion to their longing, whereas people who have little or
no desire to share will receive little or no Light. Therefore, a person with little desire to share would not be

entirely wrong in stating that there is no Creator or grand design, because for them these do not exist.

The true measure of a person's worth lies not in the magnitude of inborn desire, but rather in how positively or negatively he or she implements inherent aspirations. No amount of ambition, if it is rooted in the negative aspect of desire, can lead to spiritual fulfillment. By transforming the negative aspect of desire into the positive aspect, however, work can have the effect of challenging a person to reach his or her full spiritual, emotional, and intellectual potential.

Imbalance

The desire to receive — which, as we have seen, was originally created for the sole purpose of drawing down the endless blessing of the Creator — is all too often transformed on our physical level of existence into a desire to receive for the body alone, without any thought of sharing. A great desire to receive is not in itself harmful to the extent that it contains a constant opportunity for an equally great desire to share. Imbalance occurs only when the desire to receive dominates an individual without restraint. In that case, only the vessels of pleasure are left, without the pure and everlasting joy of the Light. This is what the Talmudic sages meant when they wrote, "He who desires money will not be satisfied with money." In all our feverish pursuit of the good things in this life, we are apt to forget that these are merely the outward forms, or Vessels, of pleasure! Even if we have earned them by the standards of this world, the pleasure they contain is small and transient.

Cause and Effect

As the seed contains the tree, so too is the effect always contained within the cause. The end result is inherent from the inception. In the first chapter of the second volume of *Ten Luminous Emanations*, the Ari states, "Everything which is Desire on an Upper Level is Necessity on a Lower Level emanated by its Upper Cause." The Ari was speaking of cause and effect. The words upper and lower refer, respectively, to that which is closer to (upper) or farther from (lower) the source. Thus, when the kabbalist says that "not even a blade of grass exists in this world without having its roots in the phase above," he is referring to the idea that what happens at one stage is always the result of what happened one stage before.

Just as the leaf of a maple tree cannot suddenly decide one day to become the leaf of an aspen or an apple tree become an orange tree, so too must a person exist within the context of certain predestined genetic and cultural parameters. Similarly, this physical realm, *Malchut*, is the effect that is already contained within its "upper" cause.

Cause and effect must be considered to be two parts of a single entity, one contained within the other. As it is written, "He and His Name are One." The Light and the

Vessel are inseparable. Like space and time or mass and energy, cause and effect are one and the same.

Circular Concept

A "circular concept" is defined as "the balance between left and right, negative and positive, brought about by the use of restriction." The closer we become with the endless circle of creation, the closer we are to creating a circular concept with ourselves and the world around us.

People caught up in their own desires are like snakes eating their own tails. The Desire to Receive for the Self Alone causes layer upon layer of negativity to build up; the greater the desire to receive, the greater the constriction. As they recede further and further from the circular concept, such individuals become increasingly blind to the Light of Creation until the connection with the Endless Light is finally severed. Thus, with blinded eyes, they go through life unaware that the brilliant Light of the Endless is within them and all around them, and could be theirs for the asking.

Yet not all people are imprisoned by avarice. A few are free of compulsions; a few can do without habitual crutches; a few are not self-absorbed to the point of self-destructiveness; a few are not so wrapped up in negativity as to be suffocating; a few are blessed with a clear conscience. A blessed few.

Why are some of us serving life sentences in a kind of negative purgatory while others are free?

The simple answer is that some people live within a circular context — meaning that they have managed to transform the desire to receive for themselves into a Desire to Receive for the Sake of Sharing through restriction. Others, however, have not. In a similar manner, some are able to combine their balanced best interests with those of others, while others are not. The physical world is steeped in negativity, and we are all subject to its influence. We cannot escape it, but we can, through our positive thoughts and actions, turn it to our best advantage and rise to our fullest potential.

Giving and Receiving

Giving, says an old adage, makes life worth living. What could be nobler and more spiritually uplifting than helping the destitute, the hungry, and the homeless? Surely one can achieve no greater reward in life than sharing with those less fortunate than oneself. True, helping those in need can be one of life's most gratifying experiences, as can receiving what has been long sought and justly deserved. Yet it is by no means difficult to cite numerous instances in which neither the giver or the receiver derives any lasting sense of achievement.

Concerning the aspect of sharing, for instance, one is hard pressed to imagine a more thankless and futile proposition than lavishing gifts on someone who does not want, need, or deserve them. Moreover, a gift worth giving transmits something of the giver. If the giver does not experience some sense of loss or personal sacrifice, even an act of seeming beneficence is viewed, from the kabbalistic perspective, as a manifestation of greed.

Conversely, with regard to the aspect of receiving, no fulfillment other than that of the most transitory nature can be gained by receiving something that is not wanted, needed, or deserved. Consider the many sizable inheritances that have been squandered or the fortunes that have been hastily acquired and impetuously lost through gambling. Easy money has wings; it departs as effortlessly as it arrives. Nor does hard work or even sincerity guarantee protection from the pitfalls of conscience insofar as receiving is concerned. No matter how we struggle to achieve some goal, we will gain no lasting gratification if the underlying motivation is purely desire to receive for ourselves alone. This is the circumstance of people who step on the necks of others, so to speak, as they claw their way up the ladder of success. The same applies to the thief who steals millions, or to anyone who achieves wealth or high standing with no purpose other than greed, ego gratification, or material acquisition.

Mere sharing does not bring us to an altered state of consciousness. Nor does receiving necessarily impart any lasting benefit unless it is accompanied by an attitude of resistance. For the giver, resistance takes the form of giving what he or she really values and wants to retain, while the receiver, contrarily, creates a circular condition by wanting to receive but rejecting that which is offered.

The truth of these examples is seen when we examine giving as it relates to the condition that existed in the Endless World. There the state was such that the as yet undifferentiated energy-intelligences within the Endless began to feel a sense of disquiet at receiving the Creator's infinite abundance while having no ability to give anything in return. It is pointless to give unless that which one gives is well received. The Emanator felt obliged to restrict the outpouring of beneficence so as to allow the emanated the opportunity to absolve Bread of Shame. Henceforth, after the restriction, it became the prerogative of the emanated to accept the Light or not, as was so desired. This is precisely why sharing, charity, and philanthropy, in and of themselves, do not necessarily benefit either the giver or the receiver unless those acts are accompanied by restriction, which complies with the first act of creation.

Balanced Relationship

In the balanced relationship between donor and recipient, the concept of Bread of Shame is rendered void on certain specific occasions, such as one in which the traditional order of the marriage ceremony is reversed. When the bridegroom is a man of great merit owing to the study of Torah, the bride may give the wedding ring to him instead of he to her. The Talmud explains that "through his recipiency, the marriage has become legalized by her delight in being honored by his acceptance of the ring, although the legal procedure has been reversed" (*Zohar I*, p. 7a).

The important point to note here is that the significance of this act lies in the giving, the token ring or coin being of little intrinsic value. In the exceptional case we have described, however, we are forced to conclude that the bridegroom's act of receiving the ring from his bride is in itself regarded as an act of giving. Rather than giving her a coin or ring, which is a material symbol, he presents her with the far more lofty and spiritual delight of honoring her by marriage. Receiving that is undertaken for the sole purpose of sharing constitutes absolute, complete bestowal. Thus, the groom in this instance is considered by the sages of the Talmud to be giving more by receiving the ring than he would were he to give it.

There is also an equivalent heightening in the transference of spiritual energy, since by her act of giving, the bride is receiving — and, more to the point, she is receiving far more than she would have had she merely received the ring from the man. In this heightened dynamic interchange of energy, the relationship is consummated, and Bread of Shame is totally banished. When the bride gives the ring to the man, she elevates her role of recipient to that of donor and brings the necessary balance to the relationship.

Dynamic Interplay

Rav Isaac Luria stated the kabbalistic view that "the blood of man provides the link between the soul of the upper realm and the corporeal body in the terrestrial realm." The blood embodies the dynamic interplay between soul and body. Blood contains both the energy-intelligence of sharing and the energy-intelligence that is found in all other parts of the body — that is, the desire to receive for the self alone.

The discovery that blood consists of red and white cells came as no surprise to the kabbalists. Kabbalah had long designated red as the color that represents the desire to receive, while white had long been defined as a symbol of the desire to share. Blood, as the binding link between the soul and body, must, it was reasoned, contain within its molecular structure both aspects of desire. Blood unites all members of the corporeal family. When any portion of the body suffers injury, the blood demonstrates its desire to impart by rushing to the scene of the accident. The red cells embrace the energy-intelligence of receiving; the white cells, whose function is to destroy infection, demonstrate the opposite energy-intelligence, that of sharing.

Explorations into the subatomic realm in the 20th century have helped reveal the dynamic interplay within the cosmic unity. The components of an atom do not exist as isolated energy-intelligence but rather as integral parts of an all-encompassing whole.

We see the process of dynamic interplay at work every second of our lives in the mechanism by which we draw the breath of life into our lungs and then expel it. The inward breathing represents the desire to receive and the exhaling of air the desire to impart; clearly the two must be in perfect balance at all times. We also notice that we must breathe in before we can breathe out, just as we must have a desire to receive before we can share — and we cannot exhale a greater amount of air than we breathe in.

For us to capture and retain permanent spiritual nourishment or emotional satisfaction, the interplay of giving and receiving must at all times be balanced, thus enabling the Light of all-inclusive beneficence perpetually to illuminate each and every corner of our being.

Chapter VI

RESTRICTION TECHNIQUE

Kabbalah teaches that reality diminishes in direct proportion to physicality. Deluged as we are by an endless stream of sensory stimulation, we might easily be deceived into thinking that the world of appearance — the world we see, hear, taste, touch, and smell — is the be-all and end-all of existence. By challenging the material illusion, we create a circuit with the alternate universe of the mind and become channels for higher states of consciousness. That is why the kabbalist seeks not to satisfy the myriad superficial desires presented by the world of illusion, but rather to restrict them. This is true control. This, not the tyranny of material illusion, is the root of real self-determination and the way to transform life's negative polarity into the positive. Resistance to the finite material illusion is the key to unlocking the gates of the only true reality — that of the Infinite.

World of Restriction

Just as the physical veiling or screening of the light of the sun blocks its penetration, so does the whole of creation constitute an enormous process of restriction or rejection, brought about by the original restriction that took place in the Endless World. This restriction occurred during the process of creation, when it was executed as a voluntary restraint of the desire to receive. It catapulted us from infinity into creation and was only the first of untold billions of restrictions that were to follow.

To preserve the illusion of separation between Emanator and emanated, allowing us the opportunity to absolve Bread of Shame, a gap was created to put "distance" between the physical and metaphysical realms. This gap, called the Curtain, is the power that prevents Light from spreading to the fourth phase. It is not the original restriction per se, but rather a further restriction that happens only at the moment the Light of Creation reaches this, the fourth phase. In other words, the Curtain acts involuntarily to repel the Light.

As explained by the Lurianic system of the Ari, there are two modes of restriction: one voluntary and the other involuntary. The earth and all its creatures, with the sole exception of people, have a built-in limiting mechanism. The earth's primal motivating energy-intelligence, the desire to receive, acts involuntarily in conjunction with nature's inborn restrictive mechanism (the Curtain) to reveal sunlight. No light materializes other than that which is reflected. Sunlight is revealed only through a particular act of resistance (reflection). This fact becomes readily apparent when one gazes into the night sky. There is only darkness between the stars, planets, and heavenly bodies simply because there is nothing of a physical nature with which light can interact. Hence, having nothing to reflect from (other than nuclear particles that exhibit only a minute desire to receive), light cannot be seen.

Because of our wish for individuation, however, we must reveal the Light through a conscious or voluntary act of restriction so as to absolve Bread of Shame.

It is the purpose of Light to be revealed and the purpose of humans to reveal it. The aura of Light permeates every atom in the universe, yet it must remain in a potential state until people, by their conscious desire, make the necessary connection. By our restriction, our denial, we act as a filament that brings forth the Light. In this way we fulfill the purpose of both Light and Vessel, circle and line (the line represents this physical dimension, and the circle represents the totality of the physical dimension unified with the upper worlds). By denying the darkness, we reveal the Light; by restricting the negative, we release the positive.

No light, no sound, no thought — nothing comes to light in this World of Restriction without resistance, and the greater the resistance, the more magnanimous is the outpouring of energy. We of *Malchut* must work to deactivate the Curtain and thus reilluminate our infinite energy-intelligence.

Binding by Striking

A fire can be started by striking one rock against another to produce a spark. A similar action must take place whenever Light is brought into this world. Light emanates to this world in response to desire, but when that Light arrives, the Curtain deflects it. Light so repelled is called Returning Light, which is said to bind with the Upper Light, giving illumination to the Upper Emanations. This action is known as binding by striking.

A person's Encircling Vessel is his own potential; that is, one receives only the Light that one has the capacity to reveal. The Light never says no; that is our prerogative and ours alone. While we may want to accept the Light that is freely offered, we cannot do so without deactivating Bread of Shame.

People can bind or reveal the Light to the upper reaches of their being only by striking the Light away. If they were to receive the Light directly from the Source, neither the purpose of the Light nor that of the Vessel would be served. The Light would envelop the Vessel and the universe would revert to a circular condition, which would be contrary to the desire of the Vessel, whose

Bread of Shame originally caused the Light and the Vessel to separate.

Just as the eyes must adjust to changes in light, so must the "eyes" of the soul be prepared before gazing on the Light of the Endless, the *Ein Sof*. Just as a light bulb would be obliterated by the sudden infusion of a million watts of raw electric power, so would an unwary life force be vaporized by direct connection with the Endless Light.

The light that manifests inside a light bulb is not, as most people imagine, the result of some harmonious conversion of electricity within the filament. Rather, it is the effect produced by a violent resistance on the part of the negative pole. The negative pole, in effect, is asking the positive pole for electricity, and the positive pole, whose desire is to impart, readily complies. This brings us to a paradox: Rather than accepting the electricity it just asked for, the negative pole repels it, thereby causing the filament to heat up to red-hot intensity to reveal the light.

The brightness of a light bulb is determined solely by the size of the filament, its resistor — not by the current that runs through the wiring system. The current is the same no matter what appliance plugs into it, whether it is an air conditioner with great demands or a five-watt bulb with a minute requirement. Just as a light bulb produces only that amount of light which its filament is capable of generating, so do we manifest only the exact amount of Light that our filament (our capacity for restriction) allows our inner Encircling Vessels to reveal.

Strike one rock against another and a spark will be produced. Strike it again, this time with more force, and the spark will be larger. When we focus the light of the sun through a magnifying glass (restriction) onto a sheet of paper, the paper eventually lights up in flames. The smaller the point of focus (the greater the restriction), the more forceful the revelation or release when the paper begins to burn.

The harder we concentrate on something (restriction by blocking out other thoughts), the more notable the breakthrough in terms of our thinking. Consider the production of sound. The harder a string is struck with a plectrum, the louder the note. The greater the force of compression on a membrane, the more forceful the percussive effect.

Revelation begins with restriction.

A woman's uterine contractions precede the miracle of birth. Athletes as well as body builders have an expression — "No pain, no gain" — that attests to the exact correlation of results produced with the degree of restriction imposed on the musculature. Even on a metaphysical or thought level, we see that the same principle is valid. Concentration, or narrowing (restricting) the focus of our thoughts, is necessary to manifest words and ideas of the highest order. Where little restriction is exercised, the thoughts produced are of the "like, well you know" variety.

Art, literature, music, philosophy — no matter what the field of endeavor, the larger the capacity for restriction, the more magnanimous will be the outpouring of Light. This paradox arises even when we are doing the dishes or mowing the lawn. Sometimes, when we are bored with our work or have other, "more important" things to do, time drags by and our energy becomes so drained that productivity becomes almost impossible. Yet the moment we decide to apply ourselves to the same task, something happens. By concentrating, focusing, and restricting our focus, we release new energy, and the job goes faster — and when it is accomplished, we have energy to spare to take on the world.

Our eyes are unable to experience the Light directly, as its infinite brilliance is simply overwhelming. The only Light we see is reflected Light, which comes to us through the process of resistance. The greater the capacity for resistance, the greater the revelation of the Light. This is the first paradox as well as the root of every paradox in the universe.

Central Column

The universe operates on a three-column system. Acting between the positive Right Column, or sharing influence, and the negative Left Column, or receiving influence, is the mediating principle known to Kabbalah as the Central Column. Restriction is the energy-intelligence of the Central Column. The Central Column is analogous to the neutron in the atom or to the filament in a light bulb. The Central Column represents the mediating principle that must bridge the two polarities, positive and negative, so that energy can be manifested.

The Central Column can be likened to the moderator in a debate or to a referee, a diplomat, or the arbitrator of a dispute. Just as the filament must exercise resistance to reveal light, so must arbitrators restrain their own particular opinions or beliefs in the interests of settling conflicts. Like the intermediary, we all want to have our way — in other words, to receive for ourselves alone. The paradox is that to accomplish this, we must restrict what we want to receive — for it is only through restriction that energy is revealed.

Restriction is the energy-intelligence of the Central Column. By resisting what we want to receive, we create the connection that gives it to us. How strange this concept seems at first glance — how backward, how thoroughly wrong-headed. Can the kabbalist seriously expect us to believe that to get what we want, we must first reject it? That to arrive at yes, we must say no? Yet as strange as it may seem, the principle of Returning Light dictates a situation such that all energy revealed in this World of Restriction is reflected (restricted) energy. Hence, if we want to receive (or, in other words, to reveal the energy we desire), we must withhold our desire and thereby create a blockage to the actual receiving. The moment we say no, the Central Column creates interference in the realm of *Malchut*, and this allows the Light, the positive energy, to be revealed.

Perspectives

Students of Kabbalah generally have no difficulty understanding how the negative pole's resistance to incoming electricity initiates illumination in a light bulb. Nor do they have the slightest problem understanding the concept of resistance when confronted with some of the myriad physical examples of this phenomenon in action. All we have to do is contract a muscle (resistance) to see that it grows. Compare a reflective, light-colored surface with an absorbent, darker-colored one in strong sunlight, and no doubt will remain that the former sheds (resists) more illumination than the latter. When we strike one rock forcibly against another, the concept of binding by striking flashes to life before our eyes. Yet however easily we may accept physical examples of resistance (the Curtain) and restriction (*Tsimtsum*) in universal terms, still we struggle when attempting to apply this concept in personal terms to our daily lives.

Modern nations, cultures, and civilizations were founded and built, we are told, by men and women who believed in a philosophy of setting goals and striving toward them.

107

Every day in school, on television, and in books and magazines, we are presented with examples of people who, through their apparent dogged striving, have "made something of themselves." When at first we don't succeed, the prevailing wisdom goes, try and try again. Contrary to this, the kabbalist attempts to inform us that the greater our desire to possess something without resisting, the less likely are our chances of acquiring it. Conversely, resisting what we desire most is the surest way of getting it. It is little wonder that our personalities — knowledge perceived by the senses and learned from birth — cry out in protest of such an idea. This seeming contradiction rubs against the grain of all we have ever learned. How are we expected to "get somewhere in this world" if we reject that which we most desire?

It is one thing, after all, to look at physical examples of resistance in action, and quite another to adopt it as a way of life. One important obstacle to contend with is the bias of Newtonian physics. Newton believed that nature is governed by absolute laws that operate totally apart from human consciousness. The Newtonian perspective, acquired by all who attend our nation's schools, conditions us to believe that we can study nature without considering ourselves to be part of the equation. So seemingly universal is this misconception that it is generally accepted without question.

Kabbalah, on the other hand, teaches that we are participants in nature and therefore cannot possibly study its laws without also studying ourselves. Hence the kabbalist, merely by observing the laws that govern the external physical world (such as binding by striking), concludes that the same laws must also be acting internally within each of us. Resistance, then, being the modus operandi in the physical world, must also rule the realm of the metaphysical, including our emotional lives and even our thoughts. As basic and utterly sensible as this idea "feels" when expressed in simple terms, it still escapes the vast majority of people, precisely for the reason stated earlier — that most people perceive nature as something apart from themselves.

Given these prevailing cultural perspectives and educational conditions, it is little wonder that the student of Kabbalah cannot initially grasp — and therefore will not wholeheartedly embrace — the concept of resistance. It is not easy, after all, to break the bonds of teachings that have been so deeply ingrained. The verity of resistance, this most elusive element of kabbalistic thought, must be approached from various levels and angles — mentally, emotionally, and physically — if it is to be fully comprehended and used to our best advantage. As is the case with all kabbalistic truths, the idea of resisting what is most desired cannot be perceived by means of logic alone. It must be experienced.

Concerning this seemingly enigmatic kabbalistic concept, it should be remembered that the kabbalist asks us to reject not the Light but rather the obstruction of Light, the desire to receive for the self alone. However paradoxical this may seem, by resisting what we most desire, we create an altered state of consciousness that satisfies all desires.

Short-Circuitry

Temptation comes at us in a constant barrage. Advertising leaps out at us from billboards and television screens, luring us to buy what we do not need and cannot afford. Attractive models beckon from the glossy pages of magazines, enticing us to drink, smoke, gamble, consume drugs, and act licentiously. Some of us surrender to these temptations only rarely, while others do so regularly and still others continually. Habitual surrenderers, in contemporary cultures, are absolved of responsibility for their vices through use of a convenient (but erroneous) catchall label: "addictive personality."

Failure to restrict the negative aspect of desire produces a short circuit that causes people to remain in a state of robotic consciousness. Surrendering to the illusion perpetuates the darkness and imparts pleasure to no one. The conscience of the person who is motivated by the negative aspect of desire carries a heavy burden: the weight of illusion, the darkness, the blindness that is the constant companion of Desire to Receive for the Self Alone. kabbalists, on the other hand, have no excess freight to carry; their consciences are clean and their vision unobstructed.

The illusion is given weight and substance by our thoughts and actions. By accepting the illusion as our reality, we make it real. The thief sustains the illusion, as does the cocaine baron, the inside trader, and all those who better themselves at the expense of others. The person who succumbs to the negative aspect of desire perpetuates the illusion, whereas kabbalists, by their resistance, destroy the illusion and reveal the Light.

The difference between the kabbalist and the person who is motivated by the negative aspect of desire is that whereas the latter — the thief, the inside trader, the greed-motivated businessperson — attempts to achieve fulfillment by satisfying the Desire to Receive for the Self Alone, the kabbalist achieves true fulfillment by rejecting that same impulse.

The material trappings accumulated by the person who is motivated by Desire to Receive for the Self Alone will be just that — traps, prisons from which the only escape is restriction. Instead of enjoyment, these trappings will bring only grief. Such a person may own many estates but may never feel at home in any of them. He or she may possess beautiful and priceless art objects, but they will impart less true pleasure than if they were graffiti scrawled on a wall. As much time and effort as the person might have expended, as difficult as any task might have been, as brilliant and incisive as his or her actions may have appeared to others, a person who is inspired by the negative aspect of desire will receive no lasting satisfaction from the spoils of greed-motivated labors.

Ironically, all of the acquisitions accumulated by greedy people cause them only greater discomfort. If the same people were to restrict and thus remove the illusion, they would acquire the contentment that so eludes them. That is the paradox of Returning Light: By saying yes to the impulse to receive for the self alone, we get nothing; whereas by saying no to that same impulse, we can, quite literally, "have it all." Nonetheless, it is a fallacy to think that money and material possessions will automatically bring us fulfillment. The only act that imparts true contentment is restriction.

Circuitry

Fulfillment exists only in the real world — the Endless World in which the Desire to Receive for the Self Alone has absolutely no influence. Desire to Receive for the Self Alone preserves the illusion; voluntary resistance destroys it. Restriction creates an altered state of consciousness to bridge the gap between the Light and ourselves.

The goal of kabbalists, then, is to redirect their thought processes in such a way as to bring about the end of the reign of the illusion, thereby restoring illumination to the world and, as a consequence, to themselves. This may seem at best a difficult if not impossible task until we understand that despite its seeming omniscience, the 1 percent world (the physical world, which represents only 1 percent of total reality) is in fact an illusion, and one that has such a tenuous existence that even the smallest degree of resistance can destroy it. Even a little resistance can illuminate a large, dark space. Light a match in a totally darkened airplane hangar, and every corner will, at least to some small degree, be exposed.

Such is the beauty of Returning Light.

Through their conscious resistance, kabbalists serve the needs of both Light and Vessel. By transforming the negative aspect of desire into the positive, they expose the illusion of darkness to the Light of reality. Light is everywhere, ready, willing, and able, at the slightest provocation (resistance), to reveal its endless presence. Through conscious resistance to the desire to receive for the self alone, kabbalists act in a manner not unlike a match in an airplane hangar or the filament in a light bulb. They establish a circuitous flow of energy, which in turn creates a wide circle of Light even from a small amount of resistance.

Experiencing Restriction

The concept of restriction needs to be understood, as it is applicable in our daily experience. To receive the benefits of the Light, one needs to restrict it, at which point an unexpected result occurs. Rather than having lost the Light because of its restriction, you have made a place for it to be received consciously and with purpose: the purpose of sharing. The direct light is too strong to be handled and would cause damage. Having done the restriction, the Returning Light will fulfill with comfort the desire to receive. In the physical world, the Light may come in the form of material value or success. Here, too, the process of restriction prepares a place for its receipt and makes certain to balance the receiving and giving.

It is important to understand that kabbalists' denial of what is desired is not done with the intention of creating personal suffering; nor is it an exercise in self-negation. Rather, kabbalists restrict what they most want precisely because they desire to receive all that life has to offer.

The amount and length of time of restriction vary according to each particular desire and differ for each individual. By using restriction in our daily lives, we learn how much resistance we need to apply to different desires. Hence, we find that even this concept of denying what is desired must be tempered with restriction, for such is the nature of the paradox of resistance.

The basic procedure is to apply restriction to our desires with the conscious thought of rejecting a particular need or want, but not to verbalize this in speech. After the energy-intelligence of restriction has been injected, a more positive outcome will be manifested into our lives than if no restriction had been applied.

Toothache Technique

The idea of resistance takes some getting used to. Today, in a modern, sophisticated society, "instant," and "new" demands have become synonymous with quality. Have a headache? "Quick, fast relief" is the catch phrase of the day. Let's face it: Who wants a lingering, painful head- ache? Yet however successful a remedy may be, the price is still only "temporary" relief. We have in effect traded permanent relief for the so-called instant benefit, thereby abandoning our inherent right to a pursuit of health and happiness.

In the desire for more pain lies the removal of pain.

This metaphysical paradox goes against the grain of con- temporary popular culture. Undoubtedly it will be some time before it is understood, much less accepted, by those who refuse to let go of their illusory lifestyles.

Take, for example, the common toothache. At the on- set of pain, we have been programmed to immediately begin popping pills in the hopes of acquiring temporary relief. And when the pain returns, we revert back to popping again.

How do kabbalists react to a toothache? At the first hint of pain, they are overjoyed by this unique opportunity to restrict the demand of that negative pole — the illusory physical body — for instant relief and fulfillment. They know the benefit of pain, its cleansing and therapeutic cure for some of their personal correction.

Who does, in essence, feel pain if not our corporeal body? It demands energy to erase the lack of physical well-being. Essentially, pain is the warning signal that our free-flowing energy system has been disrupted. However, if we were to react to this universal demand for "things for nothing" without restriction, we would inevitably suffer the consequences of the poor light bulb. When the filament permits the negative pole to make its simple demands for electrical current and the filament is either asleep or nonfunctional, a short circuit develops.

What seems to emerge from our insights into reality is that there are two opposite ways to deal with pain. While awaiting professional assistance to remove their pain, kabbalists, for their part, are enjoying their illusory misfortune. Who knows; they might actually restore their systems to a circuitry of energy by means of their art of restriction.

The usual toothache sufferer, meanwhile, is frantic and in pain, popping pill after pill until relief arrives. Then who knows what might be in store for him?

Conscious Restriction

Of all the creatures in this world, only the human lacks an instinctive restrictive mechanism. Before the original restriction, you will remember, we asked for and received a degree of free will that allows us to reveal the Light or not to do so, as we so desire. We must either consciously reenact the restriction, and in so doing absolve Bread of Shame, or succumb to negativity and remain in darkness. Light never diminishes - only the capacity for restriction.

By our conscious restriction, we reveal the Light. If we choose not to restrict, we allow for the existence of darkness. Those who fail to exercise the option of restriction place themselves at risk of being inundated by the Curtain's negative influence. They allow the Curtain to arbitrarily choose when, where, and how much Light the vessels will or will not receive. But those who restrict voluntarily have control over the power of the Curtain and are virtually impervious to its negativity. Not exercising restriction imprisons us in a state of psychological, emotional, and spiritual emptiness and longing. When viewed from this kabbalistic perspective, the choice presented to humanity on this phase of existence boils down to one absurdly simple solution:

Restrict so that the Light may be revealed.

We and we alone can act as filaments between the Light of the Endless and the Encircling Vessels that are within us and all around us, striving for revelation.

Conscious restriction is not required on the part of the earth, the moon, or other planetary objects in order to reflect the light of the sun. Nor is a body of water or any other physical object compelled to voluntarily reflect sunlight so that light may be revealed. Light reflects from a mirror without the mirror's conscious intervention. The filament repels electricity with no act of awareness. Only humanity must exercise voluntary resistance to reveal the Light. Failure to restrict or otherwise reflect the Light that is freely offered can result in enmity, financial disaster, lack of order and communication, obesity, alcoholism, and a host of other problems. Voluntary resistance, on the other hand, allows us to fulfill our true purpose, which is to achieve affinity with the Light through the removal of Bread of Shame.

Kabbalists resist what would take them from their mission to restore the Light. They repel temptation, obstruct deception, and deny illusion. They restrict pride and vanity, resist fraud and duplicity. They narrow their frames of reference to the root cause, the primal essence of existence — for only from the perspective of the source can all future emanations be seen.

To focus is to restrict, and to restrict is to create affinity with the Creator. The longer and more attentively we restrict our focus to the physical or metaphysical manifestation on which our sights are set, the greater will be the probability of successful completion. By consciously reenacting the creative process of the original restriction, we rekindle the ancient spark of infinity.

Just as there is no light in the cold, dark reaches of space because the light has nothing there to reflect off, so do the dark places in the consciousness of humanity remain in darkness until positive resistance is exercised. Conscious, positive resistance is the mediating principle between the positive and negative aspects of our existence. Resistance reveals the Light, which obliterates darkness. The paradox is that by resisting the Light — the gift we most desire — we receive it.

In this World of Restriction, which is also the world of revelation, it is a physical and a metaphysical truth that the greater the degree of resistance, the brighter the revelation of Light.

Chapter VII

CONTROL YOUR DESTINY

The laws regarding the flow and transfer of metaphysical energy, from which all physical manifestations grow, were established in the process of creation. These laws include the reasons we are present in this physical world and are subject to the desires we experience. What is established by voluntary means on a high level, however, becomes involuntary on successively lower levels. This is similar to a law established by a government's process of debate and decision that subsequently becomes binding on all its citizens.

The freedom our souls chose voluntarily by restricting the Light of the Endless was intended to give us the opportunity to redress the imbalance between what we were receiving and what we could give to others. While we can exercise our desire to receive for our own gratification without any thought of sharing with others, the essential structure of the universe (Bread of Shame, restriction) applies. Gratification, whether spiritual or physical, will last only if there is a balance between receiving and sharing.

If we examine our desires for the physical benefits of this world, we find that they all stem from this same root: the lack of fulfillment. Whether our desire is for money, status, or possessions, the common element is always the desire to receive, an awareness that we have lost, a fulfillment we once had, and an idea that we can regain by amassing physical objects. We have lost sight of the true purpose of our existence on this physical level so that the desire to receive is directed toward things other than the Light, which is the desire to share.

The thought behind creation was to share. The effect of this motivating cause was the creation of humanity as a Vessel for that bestowal, thus revealing our true essence as the desire to receive, the vital pivot of creation.

Only through a complete understanding of the desire to receive in all its manifestations will we attain a better understanding of our inner motivating consciousness and its relationship with our physical actions — and, more important, a better understanding of our relationship with everyone we meet along life's road.

To Reveal or Not to Reveal

Before the great restriction, we, the emanated, asked for and received the eternal and inalienable aspect of free will that allows us to reveal the Light or not, as we so choose. The Light that once filled our inner Encircling Vessels restricted and withdrew, but certain "impressions" or "residues" remained in them. These echoes of our former completeness allow us to find no rest, no fulfillment, until the now seemingly vacant Vessels again sparkle with Light.

We believe that our actions initiate results that inventors invent, that composers compose, that discoverers discover. According to kabbalistic philosophy, this is a fallacy. Kabbalah teaches that the most anyone can hope to do is reveal what already is. As the old saying tells us, there is nothing new under the sun. Everything that ever was or will be must of necessity have been present in the Endless before the Thought of Creation. The seeds of all ideas and inventions, great and small, are therefore around us and within us, awaiting revelation. Thus, by aligning our thoughts and actions with the needs of our time, we can make ourselves worthy of being channels through which some truth or great discovery might be expressed.

Cosmic Activity

Humankind was created on the sixth day or period of the Creator's creative process. Why was this creation saved

for last? Because we are the culmination of all that pre-
ceded. We are an excellent draft and skeleton of the entire
cosmos. In addition to being participators, humanity was
given the opportunity to become determiners of universal
and galactic activity.

The Zohar maintains that our internal activities can
determine external events. Our thoughts influence and
are inseparable from the external world. A similar view
is expressed in the "participant observation" theory of
quantum mechanics, which maintains that observers
cannot possibly separate themselves from what they are
observing. This theory also negates the idea of a clear-cut
division between events, physical objects, and human
consciousness.

A key element of the Zoharic worldview — one could
almost say the essence of it — is the concept of the unity
and mutual interconnectedness of all aspects and events.
To consciously perceive and embrace the union of all of
the universe's myriad manifestations is to experience the
highest reality.

For as man's body consists of members and parts of various ranks, all acting and reacting upon each other so as to
form one organism, so does the world at large consist of
a hierarchy of created things, which when they properly
act and react upon each other together form literally one
organic body.

Zohar I

The preceding verse stresses the intimate connection between the cosmos and us. *The Zohar* abounds with references to the dominant role played by humankind in achieving a mastery of our destiny and the improvement of our quality of life. It places religion in a context of spiritual experience rather than one of rigid, reactionary adherence to dogmatic doctrine for the sake of Deity. As portrayed by the *Zohar*, humankind is a spiritual entity whose fate is determined by the nature of its thoughts and actions. Only humankind has the option to exercise free will when it comes to its own spiritual evolution.

Growth

What causes growth? Why do seeds become trees? Why is the physical universe expanding? In a word, the answer is desire. Desire draws energy to itself. The only time there is a lessening of expansion is when there is a lessening of desire.

Growth is something we share with all things physical. Spiritual and intellectual growth is our only method of relieving the burden of Bread of Shame. Physical birth, growth, and death, according to kabbalistic wisdom, are of consequence only in the realm of the illusion. The death of the body's desire has no effect whatsoever on the soul, whose striving and spiritual growth must continue through various lifetimes until the soul's corrective process is completed.

This process is one of restoring the soul to its true unity, thereby creating a balance in the cosmic universe. The purpose of our being here is to fulfill ourselves.

Learning to share, or rejecting greed that says "take it all," is the soul's mission in life — and in life after life after life, depending on the soul's progress toward that goal. Attaining that goal is called making a *tikune*, or correction, of the soul.

When a soul is permitted to sojourn in the physical world, it is given an opportunity to correct misdeeds perpetrated in previous lifetimes. Only the soul provides the force that can integrate body energy into the whole and convert the whole to a "Desire to Receive for the Sake of Sharing." When that occurs, the soul has fulfilled its destiny by balancing its *tikune*.

When pain, suffering, and tragedy attend us, it is only because we have mandated them in this or a previous lifetime and must now remove the defects they represent so that our souls can progress. There is no such thing as punishment in the *tikune* process; the sole purpose of that process is to move a soul toward purification. Thus, from a kabbalistic standpoint, all forms of pain, suffering, illness, and injury have their origin in the *tikune* and are there to promote growth. If the soul becomes aware of its defects and brings itself into alignment with the forces of the universe and the cosmic truths of unity, the effects of pain and suffering can be prevented or, having started, can be modified.

The soul comprises both a male and a female aspect. Marriage is an opportunity for two imperfect individuals to help each other discharge their respective *tikune* debts and advance their spiritual undertakings. There are circumstances under which a soul will return to this earth solely for the purpose of helping someone else grow and fulfill the purpose of his or her incarnation. In addition, some few souls at the fall of Adam and Eve (who contained all male and female souls, respectively, before the fall) escaped the corruption of the "evil shells or husks," and from time to time they will appear to guide us along the perilous way of our lives.

Success

Of all the life forms and energy-intelligences in the animal, vegetable, and mineral kingdoms, humankind alone is subject to the snares and entanglements created by false desires stemming from the impure, linear illusion — for only we have been given the opportunity and the responsibility for alleviating Bread of Shame.

How is it that some people seem impervious to their failures while others are totally debilitated by them?

No thought, deed, or endeavor will ever succeed on anything other than an illusory level if it is based on the impure aspect of the desire to receive. Those ventures that
are motivated by false desires lead inevitably to failure.
Therefore, one may look at almost any failure, defeat, or
lack of attainment and instantly conclude that it was born
of an impure (false) cause.

Yet personal failures should not necessarily be looked
upon with regret. Instead, they can be viewed as lessons
or as opportunities for correction — reconnecting mech-
anisms in the circle of spiritual adjustment, transformation, and reincarnation. There is only one true criterion
for the measurement of success or failure, and that is
how well one succeeds in determining and applying the
singular activity by which each of us re-creates affinity
with the Light.

Those who measure themselves according to standards
prescribed by others — by the media, by the educational
system, by conventional societal dictates, or by the
narrow precepts imposed by dogmatic religious beliefs
— are far more apt to suffer as a result of failure than are
those who measure success and failure according to their
own unique requirements. Inevitably, those who succeed
must meet certain personal prerequisites, but certainly
these have little or nothing to do with the conventional
injunctions foisted on us by the illusory material dream.
It means nothing to succeed according to the standards

of others if we do not also succeed according to our own ethics and principles.

The moment we acknowledge a failure as something other than a lesson and an opportunity for correction, we give it credence and establish it as a reality. And so we find that measuring ourselves against the standards set by others makes us immediately susceptible to this debilitating syndrome. Kabbalah teaches that we should never see ourselves as lacking in anything, for the very acknowledgment of deficiency creates deficiency, just as the acceptance of failure establish failure. Is it not more prudent and desirable to avoid as much as possible the debilitating carousel of self-deprivation that revolves around false comparisons?

Listening

What we hear depends largely on how we listen. In addition, what we are able to perceive has little to do with the words that are spoken. For example, some people have the unfortunate tendency to try to manipulate everything they hear so as to make it fit a certain ideology or obsession to which they are habitually or selfishly tied. These people are not really listening, so they do not really hear.

All sound, because it is ephemeral, is considered from the kabbalistic perspective to be illusory. As with all that is of this World of Action, however, sound also embodies a large measure of infinity. If we listen intently — if our desire to receive is properly aligned and focused, and if we make no attempt to manipulate the sounds that we are hearing so as to fit a selfish preconception — then there is no reason we might not find delight in virtually any sound, from the babbling of a brook to the ranting of an idiot or even the barking of a dog.

This is why it is possible for a wise man to listen to the words of a fool and hear wisdom while another man, who may possess a genius IQ but who is motivated only by Desire to Receive for the Self Alone, may sit for years at the feet of an intellectual or spiritual master and not understand a single word. For the kabbalist, every sound holds the potential for union with the highest states of his or her spiritual existence.

Connecting Principle

The kabbalistic philosophy regarding Torah commandments and rituals is best described by a story told more than 2000 years ago by Hillel, the great first-century scholar and teacher. A recent convert to Judaism came before Hillel and asked if it was possible to be taught the entire Torah while standing on one leg. Hillel replied, "That which is hateful to you, do not do unto your neighbor. This is the entire Torah. The remaining decrees and commandments are but a commentary on this basic principle" (Talmud Tractate Shabbat, p. 31a).

The convert's request refers to the ultimate objectives of Torah: the termination of the path along which deeds and service lead. Therefore, Hillel chose the one precept of "love your neighbor" as the specific idea that can guide us to this final goal. This precept reveals the inner spirituality of the individual — the incarnation of the truly divine within us — and thus draws us closer to the source of Light and beauty. This source, which we have called the desire to share, is the chief characteristic by which we can come to know the Creator.

We learn from the Book of Genesis that "the inclination of man's heart is evil from his youth" (Genesis 8:21). This refers to the desire to receive, which until the age of religious majority dominates all actions in the guise of a desire to receive for the self alone. The actions of a child are motivated by this essence.

Upon reaching the age of 13 years for a boy and 12 for a girl, the individual is incarnated with a good inclination, which is a potential metaphysical form of energy similar to the Creator's desire to share. From that age onward, the concept of loving your neighbor becomes the link connecting all that exists in the celestial heights with the lower level of this world.

Union

We are the channel through which the Creator's beneficence and grace flow from the upper heavenly spheres to the corporeal world. The degree and intensity of this union, however, depend on the extent to which human egocentricity transforms itself into the desire to share, since the nature of a channel or cable is to transmit energy, not to absorb it.

We can compare this to the result of placing a curtain in front of the light of the sun: The thicker the curtain, representing the desire to receive, the more the light will absorb into itself. Conversely, the thinner the curtain, the less obstruction there will be to the passage of the light. It should be clear from this example that the thinner curtain has a greater affinity for the original source of light, the sun. Although the thin curtain has no light of its own, it nonetheless has an aspect of the desire to impart (also the essential quality of light) in that it does not hinder the passage of the light. Through its absorption of light, however, the thick curtain takes on the opposite characteristic, the desire to receive — thus bringing about a separation of function between it and the sun.

Love of people — or, for that matter, love of the Creator — is not merely a theoretical concept but rather a path of life through which the spiritual can be permanently united with the earthly, thus liberating the true nature of humankind. It is not a teaching of austerity or asceticism, against which the sages often warned. We are not required to relinquish all material possessions and physical comforts in order to achieve spiritual growth. Indeed, within the framework of the physical world, this union is realized more effectively through social intercourse and commitment to society than through seclusion and self-denial, as Hillel implied in his answer to the convert.

The literal meaning of the Hebrew word for union, *dvekut*, reveals the very essence of our relationship with the Creator and other human beings. It implies attachment, a cleaving of two; while appearing to be a complete unit, each retains individual characteristics. The Torah uses the same root to describe the relationship between a man and a woman — a union that is considered to make both parties whole in that each brings what is lacking in the other to the relationship. The root of *dvekut* is "attach." It is used to portray this relationship between man and woman as well as our union with the Creator.

In working toward the ultimate objective of union — the gradual transformation of receiving for oneself into receiving in order to share — those precepts concerning our relationships with other human beings are more likely to lead to this goal than precepts concerning our relationship with the Creator. This is due to our ever-changing role and position in the daily demands of existence. The differentiation of desires that we find in our dealings with those around us forces us to explore in real terms the meaning of loving our neighbors and to recognize the diversity that has existed since the Endless World. Through this diversity, we shall eventually remove the aspect of Bread of Shame and return to the Endless.

In the process of spiritual elevation, all people are obliged to express their innermost potential of giving (and therefore, as we have understood, of receiving as well) so as to achieve their own elevation, which permits the ultimate measure of beneficence and fulfillment from the Creator. Stated in simple terms, the precepts that regulate the interactions of people are the ideal conditioning agents for transforming our basic character. These precepts are designed specifically to realign the selfish aspect of desire with the intention of the Creator, whose fundamental characteristic is that of sharing.

Thus we find in the concept of union a central virtue by which each individual — and hence humankind as a whole — can reach his or her objective in this world: that of transmuting our elemental characteristic into the fundamental characteristic of the Creator.

Candlemaker

In the higher worlds, the soul experiences both the beneficence of the Endless and the feeling of shame that results from the inability to impart anything to the all-inclusive Infinite. Thus the soul descends to this world to erase the feeling of shame and thereby achieve fulfillment. Owing to the influence of the evil inclination, however, the soul forgets its purpose in passing into this world and becomes distracted by the earthly delights of this mundane existence.

In this connection, the story is told of a poor man who found himself unable to support his family. One day, a friend told of an island so far away that it took a year to reach by boat, where diamonds were said to be so plentiful that he would be able to bring back enough to last him a lifetime. After consulting with his family, the man decided that the difficulties of the journey and the pain of separation from those he loved would be amply compensated by the rewards he could bring back, and so he embarked on a boat bound for this wonderful island.

When the boat eventually landed, he found that his friend's report had been true: Diamonds lay in great heaps wherever he looked. Quickly he set about filling pockets, bags, and boxes with the precious stones, but he was interrupted by a man who informed him that there was no need to make such haste, since the boat was not due to return for another year. It now became clear to the traveler that he would have to find some means of earning a living during these six months, since the diamonds he had collected, being so common, were of no value in this land. He made several inquiries and discovered that wax was a rare and precious commodity here, and that a man with the patience and skill to make candles would surely flourish.

Sure enough, he was soon proficient in making candles and earned enough for a good and comfortable life on the island, only occasionally thinking with sorrow of the family he had left behind. When the time came to leave after two years, he packed a case full of his most precious possessions and set off for his homeland. When he finally reached his native shores, he was greeted rapturously by his friends and family, to whom he proudly displayed the fruits of his labor — a pile of worthless candles. "I forgot," he said.

So it is with the souls who descend into this world to correct the imbalance of receiving and sharing through the application of restriction, but who forget this spiritual purpose and become preoccupied with the needs of the body and of this transient physical world.

Most people are involved only on the physical level of existence, with its ever-changing environment of effects and movement. It is easy to see how the apparently varied and complex interactions of the physical world can distract the soul from its true purpose, just as the poor man was distracted from his true purpose by the necessity of earning a living.

Sympathetic Vibrations

Every vessel has a certain note that causes it to reverberate louder than at any other frequency. We can run a moistened finger around the rim of a wineglass to find that vessel's resonant harmonic. The singer's trick of breaking wine glasses is accomplished by singing that particular pitch at a volume sufficient to cause the glass to shatter.

The same can be said for the Vessel that is our soul. One note, one activity, one calling more than any other, can cause our interior Encircling Vessels to come alive with sympathetic vibrations — the same resonant harmonic that once filled our Encircling Vessels when we were all but undifferentiated aspects of the universal music of the spheres. Finding this one resonant harmonic is the key to contentment and satisfaction.

Chapter VIII

MIND OVER MATTER

When Abraham gazed up at the stars, he foresaw that he would not have children. The Creator then told Abraham to look at the stars no longer — that he would have a son if he attached himself to the upper realms and not to the celestial bodies. While external forces influence us, we also possess the power to transcend their influence. The stars impel, but they do not compel. It is possible to remove ourselves from the influence of the celestial bodies and even to transcend external constraints. All things physical and metaphysical, including humanity, are made up of two aspects — one finite and the other infinite. The kabbalists' task is to rise above normal, rational consciousness. This means removing themselves from the confines of physicality so as to connect with the infinite upper realm.

Quantum

A dark cloud looms on the horizon of classical scientific thought and theory. New findings in the field of quantum mechanics challenge the scientific method and threaten to evaporate a mirage that has generally been accepted as reality for centuries. Physicists are now saying that we should consider the Cartesian paradigm — the foundation for modern science that acknowledges as real only what is subject to scientific verification — to be ineffective. Today, scientists acknowledge that the consciousness of the experimenter cannot be separated from the experiment. We live in a world that some say is shaped and possibly even initiated by the power of thought.

Newtonian and Einsteinian physicists must now, in light of quantum discoveries, confront the proposition that there is no such thing as true objectivity in any but a limited frame of reference. This, needless to say, strikes deep into the heart of the Cartesian paradigm, the dominant mode of Western consciousness. Objectivity is possible only when one can remain a safe distance from what is being objectified. When one is dealing with the subatomic spectrum, however, the experiment and experimenter operate as a single entity (or process); one cannot be disengaged from the other. The experiment thus becomes an extension of the experimenter, and the results of the experiment are strangely dependent on the experimenter's thoughts. Hence we find a situation in which the standard modus operandi of science is rendered invalid.

To the careful observer, the quantum phenomenon would appear to represent a trend toward a return to metaphysical values. In many ways, it seems to foreshadow the weakening of the centuries-old grip by which science has dominated its inventor — us.

The kabbalists have long known that thought not only determines the nature of the earthly reality we choose to create, but also molds the way in which we choose to interact with it. That self-created, tacitly agreed-upon reality is the field on which we play out our cycle of correction. According to Kabbalah, however, there is, in addition to this tumultuous "reality," another timeless, spaceless reality that operates according to an infinite set of criteria, beyond the machinations of the physical world. This is the reality to which the kabbalist aspires.

Kabbalists have always engaged in what has popularly come to be known as the power of mind over matter. Rather than being a mere participator, the kabbalist uses the power of thought to act as a determining agent of both physical and metaphysical activity.

The kabbalistic conception of mind over matter does not necessarily correspond or comply entirely with the popular connotation of the subject. Although certainly within the realm of practical possibility, telekinesis — the physical movement of objects through the power of thought alone — is not, to the kabbalists' way of thinking, a worthy pursuit. To the contrary, kabbalists believe that to engage in such activities is to play into the hands of the Cartesian paradigm. What, after all, is the purpose of bending a key or guessing symbols on a card if not for self-aggrandizement, for entertainment, or for the purpose of "proving" the power of mind over matter to some so-called objective observer (who we now find is objective only within a limited, physical frame of reference)?

When kabbalists speak of mind over matter, they are speaking of undergoing an alteration of consciousness from the rational, logical mode to the nonrational, "cosmic" mode that allows for the transcendence of physical constraints. Thought can traverse great distances and can affect people and objects, and it is indeed a tangible factor in the world around us.

By consciously connecting with our infinite aspect, which is done by paying constant homage to the original act of creation that is restriction, it becomes practicable for us to transcend time, space, and matter. Along with this comes the potential for telepathy, astral travel, and the instant alleviation of physical and mental pain and suffering.

Astral Projection

Legions of people of all ages and from all walks of life have reported out-of-body experiences. In fact, we have all engaged in astral projection, whether or not we remember our sojourns into the celestial realms. Science, however, has no way of validating astral projection or any other so-called mystical experience, because the phenomenon of out-of-body travel, like quantum reality, cannot be grasped by means of the scientific method. Given the inherent rigidity of his or her consciousness, the scientist is thus forced to conclude that astral projection does not exist. Yet for the countless people who have experienced astral travel, there is no question of its existence.

Not everyone, of course, has total recall of every one of his or her sublimely liberating out-of-body experiences. Quite naturally, then, those people are apt to remain unconvinced as to the mind's ability to temporarily bypass cause-effect relationships and to connect with higher levels of consciousness. For those who have no direct experience with (or simply no recollection of) the uncharted regions of consciousness, consider the power of staring with full attention at the back of a stranger's neck. The subject will almost invariably react, and often will even turn to look directly at the power source from which the beam of thought originated.

Influence

As we move up the scale of life through the mineral, vegetable, and animal kingdoms, we find an increasing desire to receive. As small as the energy-intelligence of a rock may be, it can still have influence, causing a stirring in the energy-intelligence of a person if he or she is susceptible. A desire to receive for the self alone can render a person susceptible to the negative influences inherent in

143

the energy-intelligence of that rock. Conversely, a strong Desire to Receive for the Sake of Sharing can allow a person to come under more positive influences or not be influenced at all, depending on the best interests of the person involved.

If anyone has trouble believing that a rock can influence a person, consider the men and women who have died while climbing Mount Everest. Why do people climb a mountain? The standard answer is, "Because it's there." The kabbalist would answer, "Because my energy-intelligence has an affinity with its energy-intelligence." In effect, these are two ways of saying the same thing. Many a climber has talked with a mountain, and many a mountain has answered. It is just that climbers have no words to describe the experience, so they must rely on the standard reply.

Still not convinced? Consider that our literature, films, and television are filled with wild-eyed men and women who have succumbed to the negative influences of the energy-intelligences of diamonds, gold, and precious stones. Remember the thousands of lives lost in the gold rushes of San Francisco and the Klondike? Some have killed for a single stone, while others have spent half their lives in prison.

The Light contains an energy-intelligence of positivity. The further we are removed from the Light, the closer we are to the power and influence of negativity.

Altered States

The rational, reasoning mind accounts for but a minuscule portion of our true mental potential. Most Western educators place great emphasis on mindless regurgitation of facts, tests, grades, and IQ examinations (all of which are concerned only with the rational mind). By far the greater measure of mental aptitude rests hidden, dormant and unrevealed until such time as the higher realms of consciousness are aroused and reilluminated.

The transcendence of normal, rational thought consciousness is a basic human need. The conscious, rational mind is a trap — a prison from which our higher consciousness knows it must escape. Our Encircling Vessels are crying out constantly to be delivered from this world of illusion and to be reunited with the Light. Transcendence of this dense world is as basic as eating, as natural as walking, as necessary as the elimination of bodily waste.

For kabbalists, being in an altered state of consciousness means connecting with the Endless Light for the purpose of "seeing what is born." By transforming the Desire to Receive for the Self Alone into a desire for the sake of sharing through conscious restriction, we can conquer the negative aspect of desire and achieve an altered state of consciousness that is above and beyond the negativity of this phase.

One Step Beyond

The concept of making a living can hide a multitude of emotional insecurities. It can be used as a justification for a stockbroker or other professional to work 90 hours a week and rarely see his or her family. It can give us a reason to remain in a job that is neither enjoyable nor challenging. It can allow us to be obstinate and unforgiving and can absolve us from being complacent and emotionally unresponsive.

Did the Creator place us here to engage exclusively in hand-to-mouth survival? Is material acquisition a fitting foundation on which to build a life? Are we merely slaves to the system, gears in government or corporate machinery, cogs in the wheels of progress? Is life nothing more than a string of days for mindlessly, dutifully trudging through? Kabbalah teaches that there is no such thing as a victim of circumstance; if we are victims, it is of our own minds, our own patterns of thinking and perceiving.

If we get caught up in the physical illusion, we cheat ourselves out of the better part of life. Like talking without listening, eating without tasting, or reading the words in a book without making any attempt to understand their meaning, to accept only what is presented to us on the physical level is to negate reality in favor of an illusion.

Because our physical aspect is destined to struggle for survival in the World of Action, it does not mean that we have to accept this linear physical world as the be-all and end-all of existence. We contain, after all, an aspect of infinity. The better part of us is continually connected with the infinite energy-intelligence of the cosmos. The fact that our five senses are not aware of this cosmic connection is of consequence only in terms of our limited perceptions; it has nothing to do with the infinite picture, the grand scheme of things. By seeing our actions within the context of the great universal network, we create affinity with the circle of creation.

We are what we think. If it were possible to deal only with the physical aspect of existence — which, fortunately, it is not — life would be a one-dimensional and utterly boring grind. By traversing the negative space between ourselves and our true circular nature, we reveal the Light. Through resistance, we bridge that gap, in effect squeezing out the negativity that fills the empty spaces. Thus we complete the circuit of our own fulfillment and come to the realization that the real world is one step beyond.

Chapter IX

BACK TO
THE FUTURE

The thread of our lives is woven into the entire fabric of infinity. We have the capability to trace that line backward or forward, traversing time and space, leaping from one age or one lifetime to the next at the speed of thought. For the kabbalist, past, present, and future are indistinguishable aspects of a grand infinite continuum. The real world is unified. There is an aspect of unification within the atmosphere, within us, and within everything that exists in this world.

Kabbalah teaches us a way to remove ourselves from the spiritually impoverishing cycle of negativity, struggle, failure, and ultimate defeat — which is what people stuck in the consciousness of limitation consider death to be. It leads us to a state of mind in which we are connected with the infinite continuum, where everyone and everything is interconnected, where here is there and then is now.

Most recently, physicists have become obsessed with trying to unify or find connections among the known fundamental forces of nature. The Ari already set forth the teachings of a grand unification theory. Kabbalah taught that the ten *Sefirot*, or ten energy forces, expressed and made manifest the all-embracing unified force known as the Light. All subsequent physical manifestations were and are the direct result of a universe that started out with ten dimensions.

Consequently, when the Ari presented his doctrine of motionless, timeless Light, he essentially advanced the theory that Light was the all-pervading, constant element of the all-embracing, unified whole. Therefore, connecting with and tuning into this integrated, intergalactic network system provided instant consciousness of the entire universe.

Energy-intelligences transcend space, time, and motion. Only our finite aspects are caught up in the quagmire of illusion. Our circular aspects are always connected with the great Circle of Infinity, which is not susceptible to the friction and pitfalls of finite existence. Communication between energy-intelligences is instant, transcending both space and time.

Space Walk

Above the atmosphere, beyond the realm of gravity, everything becomes weightless. In space, any physical object, given even so much as a modicum of momentum, will continue to move until such time as it falls under the influence of another, larger planetary body. In fact, removed completely from any gravitational influence, the object in question could travel for light-years without changing direction or speed.

If the earth were all dry land and a person wanted to walk around the globe, the journey would take months. Up in space, where the earth's gravitational pull is only slight, a person in a space suit could orbit the globe in little over one hour. This "physical" fact is indicative of a more significant metaphysical idea.

As with any physical object on earth, the human body is subject to gravity, which is the manifestation of the earth's primal motivating influence, desire to receive for itself alone. The soul, however, operates beyond gravity's jurisdiction and hence is free to travel in its quest to complete the cycle of correction, or *tikune*. Thus, while the body's natural inclination is to succumb to gravitation and remain inactive and rooted to one spot, the tendency of the soul is to travel in its quest for restoration with the infinite Light of the Endless.

Someone removed from the clutches of gravity would be able to travel great distances in little time. By transcending the desire to receive for ourselves alone, we are able to connect with an altered state of consciousness, which is spiritually comparable to a weightless condition. Our consciousness is no longer anchored by the limitations of time, space, and motion.

Essence of Time

Words like sooner, later, now, and simultaneous are relative expressions. What is here and now for one may be there and then for another. From the perspective of someone who is late for an important appointment, time is rushing by at a breakneck pace — whereas from the point of view of someone else who is early for the same appointment, the same time may drag along interminably. How time is perceived depends on the perspective from which it is observed.

If the person who is late for the appointment were to be suddenly teleported to his or her destination, time would immediately be transformed from an angry tyrant into a benign servant. It would be worthy of praise instead of abuse for having brought all the parties together at the same time, in the same place, for the same meeting. Distance (space) plays a part in how we perceive time.

Time, as an entity apart from the space-time continuum, does not exist. Just as height cannot exist without width, and just as depth cannot exist without the other two linear dimensions, time and space cannot exist independently. Space and time are inseparable. The clock is a human-made construct. There is no great clock from which the universe sets its cosmic watch. Nature moves according to the dictates of its own eternal yet ever-changing rhythms. Only people march in time to the beat of a clock.

While it is true that we cannot stem the tide of the space-time continuum, we can change our perception of it and, in so doing, significantly alter the course of our lives.

Imagine time as a river that runs from the far distant past into the far distant future. Imagine now that the flow of the river is controlled by your wants and needs, moods and emotions. When our thoughts are clear, so are the waters of time. When we are "agitated," the waters are also set astir. When we are in a hurry (as is someone who is late for an appointment), the banks of the river are narrow and the waters are white-capped rapids. When we are at rest, the waters run cool and calm. When we are afraid, the waters are dark and ominous. When we are at peace, the waters are mirror-like and smooth.

What, then, is the essence of time? Is it a friend or an enemy? Is it our servant — a mere convenience by which we measure our lives — or is it a tyrant who rules over us with an iron hand? Do we use it, or does it use us? There is no single answer to these questions. In the final analysis, time is what we make it.

Drums of Illusion

From the perspective of the infinite aspect of existence, the time-space continuum is an illusion. Time, as we know it, with its measured increments, may be a convenience and even a necessity in the world of illusion, but it has no merit or utility in terms of the Infinite.

Concerning the illusory nature of time, Kabbalah finds corroborating evidence in recent scientific findings. Physicists now tell us that time cannot be separated from space nor space from time — that gravity influences time, and that clocks run slower at ground level than they do high in the atmosphere. They tell us that the speed of a clock is faster when flying in one direction around the earth than it is when flying in the other. Time stands still at the edge of a black hole, and it hypothetically comes to a dead halt at the speed of light. These scientific findings, while certainly at odds with what is commonly referred to as logic and common sense, are well in keeping with the kabbalist's long-standing assertion that the common presumption of time — that of adhering to some vast, unerring universal rhythm — is in fact a complete fallacy. If time marches on, it does so to trillions of different drummers.

Space-time exists only in the lower seven *Sefirot* — the lower seven emanations of the Tree of Life. These are the dimension of the line. Only in the dimension of the line do we find hearts beating lunar cycles, biorhythms, minutes and hours, planets orbiting stars in regular-as-clock-work cycles, pulsars pulsing with uncanny accuracy, and electrons revolving around protons according to rigidly defined schedules. In fact, the entire visible universe and even much that is invisible operates in what is obviously a cyclical and measured manner. Thus, from our limited perspective, it is only natural that we view the world of fragmentation — the illusory world of time, space, and motion — as the be-all and end-all of existence. We are so used to the concept of time as a linear, never-varying absolute that even considering other possibilities requires a seemingly illogical state of mind.

Time Travel

When the kabbalist tells us that time is integrated and unchanging — that past, present, and future are all present together — we are apt from our limited perspective to consider this a logical impossibility, the domain of science fiction. Einstein himself felt that exceeding the speed of light would also mean exceeding the speed of life, as if to jump backward in time. He reasoned that since time stands still at the speed of light, it would presumably begin going backward after that speed had been achieved. In Einstein's view, this could never happen; nothing could ever exceed the speed of light. In recent years, however, there have been experiments with subatomic particles that cast doubt on Einstein's conclusions.

From our limited, finite perspective, time appears to be absolute. We are so used to gauging our perceptions according to the ticking of a clock — to the seemingly rigid schedule of birth, life, and death — that we accept the tyranny of the world of resistance as a foregone conclusion. The kabbalist asks us to remember that the Endless is beyond finite — and that by connecting with the Endless aspect of ourselves, we can throw open the gates of infinity.

Just as the seed contains the past, present, and future of the tree, so too do we embody the entire spectrum of humanity, from our earliest primordial beginnings right up to the ultimate completion of humankind. The real world is unified. Through the attitude and practice of conscious resistance, we narrow the gap in the lower seven, the dimension of time, space, and motion — which is the space between the finite and the Infinite. We then achieve an altered state of consciousness through which the time-space continuum can be transcended completely, making telepathy, astral travel, and past-life regression not mere possibilities but readily available realities.

Space

What makes a rock a rock? Consider the Rock of Gibraltar. If that rock could somehow be compressed into a state devoid of space and atoms, it would fit comfortably into a wheelbarrow. Matter is, if you will, a question of degree. The 1% of the rock that gives it shape is its energy-intelligence. The other 99% is totally oblivious to the shape of the rock and would just as soon be occupying space in a Manhattan office building, a human being, or a tree.

Space, the separation between people (mentally, emotionally, and physically), the distance between objects, even the seemingly endless void between stars and planets — all are illusions. According to Kabbalah, there is no limitation of any kind in the real world; there is no time, no space, no friction or gravity — only the eternal presence of the Endless Light. Space, then, from the kabbalistic perspective, is an apparition, albeit a necessary one. Like time, it is an illusion.

When we asked for a method by which to absolve Bread of Shame, we took upon ourselves the responsibility of revealing the Light. Only by creating the illusion of separation between the Emanator and that which was emanated was it possible to relieve Bread of Shame by reinitiating the connection with the Light. Our ability to restore this Endless Illumination depends entirely on the extent to which we can transcend the limitation, the space, the illusion of negativity that is the Curtain.

Hence, our circular, infinite selves have the potential to be in constant and instantaneous communication with all phases of the universal life force, while our physical presence falls under the influence of the Curtain. The space created by the Curtain prevents us from experiencing our true unified relationship with the world and the cosmos while prohibiting us from penetrating the vast body of metaphysical knowledge that lies hidden beneath the negative trappings of finite existence.

Being separated from a good friend or loved one is an intensely traumatic experience for some, while for others it can be nothing more than a mere inconvenience. After a year's separation, some couples return to the company of a seeming stranger while others pick up the tempo of their relationship, so to speak, without losing a beat. The difference does not necessarily have to do with varying degrees of affection. The kabbalistic interpretation of this phenomenon is that those who feel the greater sense of loss are those for whom the Curtain has greater influence.

The illusory space between the upper three and lower seven *Sefirot* in the line causes not just personal alienation but also the separation we feel with regard to the earth and the cosmos. Kabbalistically speaking, the Light is eternal, all-pervading, and never changing, while separation, space, and distance — being of a temporal nature and changing according to how they are perceived — are said to be illusions.

Release Mechanism

Through restriction, we can narrow the gap in the lower seven and thus lessen the mental and emotional space between ourselves and others. It becomes possible for our infinite Encircling Vessels to merge with the infinite Light of Creation and thus traverse infinite light-years of space in a single, instantaneous leap of consciousness.

The line is the channel by which to restore Light into our circular Vessels, reconnecting the seven of the line with the ten of the circle. Through a regimen of well-tempered resistance, we narrow the space between the finite and the Infinite, in effect squeezing out the space between ourselves and the Endless nature of the universe.

This restrictive action, known to Kabbalah as "purification of the Curtain," is the method by which the Curtain's influence is made less dense, and hence the means by which the burden of its negative influence is nullified. The student of Kabbalah should be aware, however, that because the Curtain reasserts itself continually, those who seek to lessen its darkening influence must act with equal diligence in revelation of the Light — for that is the method by which the illusion of space between our finite and infinite aspects is reduced, making it possible to merge with the circle of creation.

Speed of Light

Imagine that you are a 23rd-century astronaut and that you have a device called, let us say, a "Lightning Speedometer" that gives you a readout of the speed of light as it relates to your vehicle. Logic dictates that if you are heading toward the sun, the source of light in our solar system, the readout will be the speed of light plus the speed of your vehicle — whereas if you are heading away from the sun, the readout will logically be the speed of light minus the speed of your vehicle.

"Wrong!" cries the scientist. "Not so!" adds the kabbalist.

The scientist points to the Michelson-Morley experiment of 1886, which "proved," at least to the researchers' satisfaction (and, presumably, to Einstein's and many others' satisfaction as well), that light travels at a speed of 186,000 miles per second regardless of the motion of the observer. This means that as an astronaut, you might as well throw your handy-dandy Lightning Speedometer down the waste-disposal chute and eject it into outer space — because no matter at what speed your spaceship travels toward or away from the sun, the readout will always be the same: 186,000 miles per second!

This fascinating "fact" of science defies logic and so-called common sense. And for this reason alone, the kabbalist would dearly love to embrace it. For as the student is by now aware, one of the main reasons for studying Kabbalah lies in breaking free of the stifling net of illusion that passes for reality on this fourth phase. Unfortunately, however, the kabbalist cannot accept this concept for the simple reason that the kabbalist does not believe in the speed of light, period. As far as the kabbalist is concerned, there is no such thing. The essence of light is everywhere — timeless, all-pervading, perfectly still. Which brings us to a question that almost asks itself. If light does not move, then what is it that scientists have been measuring all these years?

Kabbalah does not entertain the possibility of the movement of light itself, which exists everywhere. It does, however, make ample room for the probability that there is movement within the light on the part of the Vessels, the *Sefirot* that act as the vehicles revealing the energy.

In this respect, the kabbalistic perspective is more in keeping with quantum mechanics, the new branch of physics that deals with subatomic particles, or packets of energy called "quanta." Quanta are more accurately described as tendencies rather than as packets or "bits and pieces" because they are not really things at all; they are rather more like Aristotle's concept of potential, which stands somewhere between physical and metaphysical reality. In any event, quantum mechanics advances several concepts that startled the scientific community when they were first introduced, one of which placed before us the possibility that certain particles travel faster than the speed of light.

Most definitely, something travels faster than the speed of light (or rather the vehicle revealing it). Thought and consciousness both have that distinct capability.

Grand Spectrum

From the kabbalistic perspective, the importance of recognizing and understanding what is reality and what is illusion lies in providing a framework for elevating our consciousness. By viewing ourselves and the world around us as interconnected, we develop and experience a greater sense of meaning and fulfillment in our lives.

When we look at a tree, we should realize that what we observe is just a single frame within its seed's original potential. As this idea enters our consciousness, we begin to see the larger picture — not just in this instance but in all other areas of life. In this way, we raise our level of consciousness.

Everything is connected. There is no space in metaphysics, no time as we know it. We are all a part of some grand space-time/mass-energy spectrum, and within every color of that spectrum, from the darkest hue to the lightest, lies the potential for influence and communication, give and take.

Chapter X

NEW AGE

Humanity has always had to fight for survival. Fourteen pounds of air pressure per square inch has been pressing down on us since the dawn of time; gravity has always created a burden for us. Since the earliest days of civilization, we have been under pressure. We have always had to struggle to make ends meet. We have psychological pressure, pressure to perform at peak efficiency, pressure to live up to the expectations of others.

Never before has this pressure, in its many forms, been so great as it is today. Now more than at any other time in history, we have stretched the thin thread of our existence to its breaking point. We have come, it seems, almost to the end of our evolutionary rope.

The world is verging on a precipice of ecological disaster. Pollution and nuclear proliferation threaten the survival of every living thing on this earth. Rape, murder, terrorism — all manner of crime is on the rise. No longer can we travel in safety; no longer is it safe to walk the streets.

Violent images come at us in a constant barrage, pushing us to the limits of emotional and psychological endurance. Stress, tension, urgency — the heat is on. The pressure cooker we call *Malchut* is about to explode.

Why is this happening now, of all times?

The Light is the source of the pressure we feel. It is telling us to realign our values to be in keeping with the new age. Now, in this Age of Aquarius, *Malchut* is under more pressure than ever before. The times demand a new social dynamic if humanity is to keep pace with technology. The greed of this phase of our evolution, the waste and rampant materialism, scream out for an outpouring of spiritual energy of equal or greater magnitude if balance is to be restored. From this day onward, no peace will come to us. There will be no rest until the Light has been revealed.

No longer can we close our eyes to the Light of Creation. The Light is pressing in, instilling in us a sense of urgency, exhorting us on to greater and greater heights of consciousness, impelling us on toward planetary consciousness.

Now more than ever, the Light of Creation demands revelation. There is only one way to relieve the pressure, and that is to reveal the Light.

Web

Humanity's rampage against nature seems all but complete. A massive, concerted, worldwide effort will have to be undertaken immediately if imminent dangers to our physical existence are to be avoided. Billions of dollars more will have to be spent to clean up the air, and still more will be needed to clean up the water. New laws will have to be enacted to prevent further plundering of land and sea. Alternatives to nuclear energy will have to be aggressively researched and developed. The problem of world hunger will have to be alleviated. And it will not suffice to relieve only one or two of these life-threatening situations — they must all be addressed. Each is so tightly interwoven with the others that the mesh is like threads of the finest cloth.

A case in point: Hunger motivates the slash-and-burn agriculture that leads to the annihilation of hundreds of thousands of acres of rain and cloud forests each year. Also known as jungles, rain forests support more than 60 percent of the earth's plant and wildlife, in addition to absorbing vast quantities of carbon dioxide and providing a significant share of the world's oxygen supply.

Ozone, a form of oxygen, is made up of a thin protective layer of the atmosphere that filters the sun's harmful infrared and ultraviolet rays. A serious depletion of the ozone layer, as will occur with the decimation of the rain forests, will cause a condition of global overheating known as the greenhouse effect, which will complete the destruction of the rain forests, melt the polar icecaps, and ultimately sound the death knell for the human race.

It has been predicted that most of the rain forests — those life-giving natural wonders that serve as precious storehouses of untold knowledge — will virtually disappear in the next quarter-century. The full consequences of our undeclared war against nature are already being felt throughout the world. Each day, several more varieties of plant and animal life disappear from the face of the earth, some not yet named much less studied. We will never know the possibilities these extinct species might have held for us — what medicines might have been distilled from them, or what tastes or aesthetic pleasures they could have provided.

Precious plant life is disappearing at an unprecedented rate, and the wholesale slaughter of animals continues unabated. Elephants are butchered only for their tusks; whales are pushed to the brink of extinction to provide a variety of products that could be better and more cheaply produced using synthetic methods. The evidence of our selfish destruction is incontrovertible, and we have run out of excuses. Now, at last, we must pay the price for our myopia and greed.

The future is here today in the air we breathe, the food we eat, the water we drink. Hardly a day goes by when we are not reminded of the dangers of acid rain, PCBs, and other pollutants. Everywhere we turn, we witness inhumanity, stupidity, cruelty, and even genocide. But at last we are beginning to understand that any serious wound to nature is a wound to ourselves — that the balance of nature is delicate and tenuous, and that everyone and everything is interdependent.

Yet understanding is not enough. Now, before it is too late, we must take immediate steps to dress the wounds of the damage already done. The hunger of Third World populations is our hunger; their pain is our pain, and their fate is ultimately our own. Only a small minority of the world's population is capable of doing anything to alleviate the world's problems, the vast majority being locked into circumstances of raw survival born of need. No longer is it sufficient for those who live in the more affluent societies to hide behind their relative comfort. No longer can we close our eyes to the havoc we have been wreaking. No longer can we plunder the earth with apparent impunity. No longer can we choose to remain ignorant of the dangers we are facing.

There was a time in recent memory when people who spoke out against technology were condemned either religious fanatics or, even worse, as enemies of progress. Technology was our savior, and it was almost a sacrilege to suggest otherwise. Proponents of nuclear energy claimed that by the 1960s we would be living a life of ease and comfort, with robots and computers taking care of all of our daily chores. Sleek, clean, nuclear-powered monorails would sweep us to our destinations. Nuclear energy, it was touted, would be ours in abundance, providing electricity to cities for a cost of pennies per day. Those bright, hopeful voices are silent now, and their short-sighted dreams of a nuclear tomorrow have dissipated into a cloud of radioactive dust.

Perhaps now the voice of reason can be heard.

Each generation has a responsibility to preceding and subsequent generations, but our burden is perhaps greater than any that our ancestors were forced to bear. Our duty is no less than to shed Light on our own ignorance so that future generations may have a world in which to live. Now, today, we must begin to look at these problems and challenges from a global perspective. Vast reserves of cosmic energy surround us — energy that so far outshines what is produced by the splitting of atoms that the comparison is like holding a penlight up to the sun. The potential energy of the Endless Light is within us and all around us, but to release those vast reserves requires an act of restriction. The initial step in creating any bridge of understanding is a conscious decision.

Comfort

We are here to make adjustments, corrections, and amendments to our finite constitutions, and these changes come about through resistance, discomfort, and suffering. Each lifetime brings us closer to our goal of one day being reunited with the great Circle of Endlessness from which we came.

The kabbalist denies the body's natural inclination, which is to remain passive, as well as the craving of the rational mind, which is to remain complacent. The simple reason for this is that the restoration of Light to the Encircling Vessels cannot be accomplished by following the directives of what is finite, including the body; it can be achieved only by obeying the infinite mandates of the soul.

Comfort, whose basic energy-intelligence is the Desire to Receive for the Self Alone, serves no purpose other than to isolate us from ourselves and from others; complacency only sidetracks us from our true mission, which is to reveal the Light. The kabbalist, then, gives thanks for the opportunity of discomfort, not to satisfy any masochistic tendencies but rather to give the soul the opportunity for correction — which is, after all, the ultimate purpose of finite existence. Self-deprivation plays not the slightest part in the kabbalist's resistance and denial.

Only by restricting the desire for comfort and complacency can the purpose of existence — the revelation of all that is real — be fulfilled. Only transitory contentment can be achieved by succumbing to the body's every whim. Thus, the kabbalist chooses the path of most resistance.

New Age

Whatever happened to the much-touted Age of Aquarius, with its promise of harmony and understanding, sympathy and love abounding? The new age is here. We are beginning to witness — and, indeed, are already participating in — a people's revolution of enlightenment. This spiritual insurrection will be made possible as a result of the efforts of individuals who are dedicated to bringing about a metaphysical understanding of the cosmos and humanity's relationship and place within it.

The prophet Jeremiah foresaw this abandonment of ignorance and its replacement by an overwhelming comprehension of the very nature of existence:

And they shall teach no more every man his neighbor, and every man his brother, saying, know the Lord; for they shall all know me, from the least of them to the greatest of them.

Jeremiah 31:34

Consciousness is a matter of revelation, a matter of simply stepping out of the darkness and into the Light. The new age was conceived in the Thought of Creation — and, like all of creation, it will be here until the cycle of creation has run its course. By our thoughts and subsequent actions, humans can change some of the footnotes of history and can slow down or speed up the process of correction — but like any finite existence, the life of the human species must of necessity have a beginning, a middle, and an end. Hence, we as a species must one day shed our physical form and merge once again with the Endless.

Ensconced as they are in the desire to receive for the self alone, some people will tenaciously cling to outmoded, violent, domineering, ego-laden frameworks of consciousness. The fact is, however, that the new age cannot be avoided. It is etched in the cosmic blueprint, the map, the DNA consciousness that was born with the Thought of Creation, and it will not disappear until the cycle of correction has come to an end. Like any living entity, the collective consciousness of humanity is destined to undergo a transformation before passing to the Great Beyond.

The only difference between the Age of Darkness in which we are living and the Age of Light that is coming is that all entities and energy-intelligences will understand their part in a universal oneness.

By way of illustration, perhaps it may be useful to imagine a scenario in which alien spacecraft suddenly threaten to exterminate all life on earth. Immediately, all petty quarrels and differences would be forgotten, and the sanctity and wholeness of the human race would rush to the surface of each individual's consciousness. Another apt comparison might be drawn between the new age

of humanity and the moments of supreme lucidity that
often precede the physical passing of an individual.

The Light is here in all of its glory; the still, timeless,
peaceful, infinite unity is present even in this world of
greed and violent upheaval. But like all things that are
real, it must remain concealed to allow us the opportunity to remove Bread of Shame. kabbalists do not cower
in fear of a coming apocalypse, hoping and praying that
they might be among the chosen few who will prosper in
the new age that is to follow. One need not, after all, look
to the future for something that is here today. kabbalists
do not gaze into the future for the beginning of the Age
of Enlightenment; they look within. The new age is here
today — as is the apocalypse, as is the pestilence, as is the
final emendation.

Trends

All things physical have their roots in the metaphysical. It
is consciousness — not science, religion, or public opin-
ion — that is the harbinger of what is to come. There is
no disappearance in spiritual substance. Nothing of value
disappears. Shapes change, appearances change, the body
changes, but the energy-intelligence never diminishes.
The illusion changes constantly, but the truth beneath
that illusion is constant and never varying. Each stage of
biological, social, and cultural evolution is impressed into
the collective consciousness. In like manner, each person's
important mental and emotional lessons are remembered

throughout the course of each lifetime, and his or her pivotal spiritual lessons are carried over from life to life. Nothing is lost. No great truths fall irretrievably between the cracks of existence; no great crimes go unpunished.

Yet we seem no nearer to resolving our problems than were our primal ancestors when they first began to contemplate the Great Mystery. Indeed, if anything, the situation seems to have worsened. With the specters of war, genocide, terrorism, nuclear proliferation, and ecological imbalance looming like dark clouds on the horizon of human consciousness, how can the kabbalist's faith and optimism remain undisturbed?

Kabbalah teaches that we must ever be wary of appearances, for things in the physical world are never what they seem. Now, as always, the physical universe gives every impression of being in a state of perpetual darkness and chaos. The Light is here, but so obscured is it by the negative trappings of finite existence that a sensitive eye and a compassionate soul are required to perceive it. kabbalists are constantly scanning the human horizon for signs of the Light's Endless luminosity. They see it in the trend toward miniaturization. Where previously a cable carried 400 conversations, a fiber-optic strand can now transfer 4000. They see it in the computer that once required a large room but is now housed in a small package that can be comfortably lifted with one hand. They see it as well in the quantum physicist's rediscovery of the so-called featureless ground state, which closely corresponds with the ancient kabbalistic contention that the true nature of reality is never changing and perfectly still.

The struggle of science to achieve more with less is seen by the kabbalist as a reflection of humans' striving to shed their garments of darkness and step once again into the Light. Thus, these developments, when seen from a kabbalist perspective, reveal an inborn tendency for people to strip from themselves the stifling remnants of physicality and to embrace the spiritual.

The astute observer can detect trends that seem to indicate a swing away from the corporeal illusion. Einstein's theories of relativity led to the reevaluation and ultimately the abandonment of rigid classical constructs involving energy and matter, time and space. Explorations into the subatomic world are revealing the dynamic interplay within the unbroken cosmic oneness.

The Light never rests. It is forever impelling us toward the culmination of the cosmic process, the re-revelation of the true reality, the *Ein Sof*, or Endless. It incessantly urges us toward that heightened state of consciousness which will allow us to remove klipot, the spiritual shells or coverings that separate us from the Light, and end the need for Bread of Shame for all time. The greater the Light's revelation, the greater is the pressure on us to reveal it. What the kabbalist sees today is an increase in pressure — a hastening of the corrective process that foretells the beginning of the end of a long, arduous process of spiritual adjustment and rectification — and the dawning, for many individuals, of a new age.

Preparation

Praiseworthy are those who will be in that age, and woe onto those people.

Zohar III, 8a–8b

A common theme in apocalyptic literature is that of the new age belonging to those who prepare for it. Some doomsayers predict that only those who have purified themselves will flourish in the new age, contending that the rest will, at best, suffer the throes of eternal damnation. When examined from a kabbalistic perspective, this same scenario is seen as having not just one but several layers of meaning.

Kabbalists always guard against literal interpretations of ancient esoteric texts, and they are especially watchful when interpreting biblical writings. This is not to suggest that a literal interpretation of the Torah does not make good reading; it does. Indeed, it cannot be denied that the Torah provides a most valuable historical record. However, the reason the kabbalist probes beneath the surface of biblical interpretation is a result of an unshakable conviction that the real meaning of the Torah is not to be found in the "outer garments" of the stories themselves.

The meaning of the Torah, like the Light, must remain concealed.

"There is not a word in the Torah that does not contain sublime and precious mystical teachings," states Rav Shimon.

Zohar I, verse 12a–12b, p. 37

The Torah, according to kabbalistic wisdom, is a cosmic code that must be deciphered. Every word, line, and passage harbors a sublime hidden meaning. Thus, to lift certain passages concerning the apocalypse and interpret them literally is, in the kabbalist's view, to engage in an exercise in futility.

Those who purify themselves have always reaped the rewards of a new age, a new life, a new level of consciousness, just as those who lurk in the shadows of negativity have always had to suffer. From a kabbalistic perspective, the age of enlightenment is not some distant, pie-in-the-sky vision of a new and better tomorrow. The new age is here, today. It begins the moment each individual chooses Light over darkness, good over bad, life over death.

As for the hellfire and pestilence predicted by some would-be soul savers, yes, that too is with us. Those who choose to live in darkness have always suffered damnation — which to the kabbalist's way of thinking is every bit as insidious as any imagined by the doomsayers. The apocalypse happens when one has reached rock bottom, when one's life is in shambles, when some wrong has been committed that must be set right. The metaphysical equivalent of hellfire and brimstone consumes the mind, the thoughts, and the consciences of those who have chosen to walk on a path of darkness. The world is strewn with the victims of self-hatred — those who have perished as a result of the atrophy of their consciousness; those who are the grim reapers of the hatred they themselves have sown.

The new age does indeed belong to those who prepare for it. Those who do not work to purify themselves must certainly suffer the spasms of self-inflicted damnation. Those who cling to antiquated, hard-line material views and values — the warmongers, the brass-tack materialists who mistake themselves for realists, the power merchants, the ego-driven prime "movers and shakers" of the physical environment — will not, without major adjustments in their spiritual modus operandi, reap the rewards of higher consciousness. And that, it seems to the kabbalist, is punishment enough.

Global Village

Kabbalists have long maintained that world unity will one day be a physical reality. In reality — meaning the infinite reality of the Light — we are all cut from the same cloth. In the grand scheme of things, we are already intimately entwined within a vast, never-changing fabric of universal peace.

Only recently has the concept of "world citizenship" reached the edge of the collective consciousness. Even here today, in this chaotic riot of insanity we mistakenly call the real world, the careful observer can perceive the emergence of a seed of changing awareness in this transitional period in humanity's tumultuous yet curiously static cultural evolution. The very fact that certain people are thinking, speaking, and even raising their voices on behalf of One World is evidence of the vast, sweeping reformation that is to come. As always, the metaphysical realm of thought is the harbinger of what will one day become reality on the physical level.

In the real, Endless World, peace already reigns supreme. As difficult as it may be to imagine, experiencing as we do only the underside of reality, it is only a matter of time (another illusory concept) before the aspiration for a united world becomes a reality here in the world of illusion.

Even today, the world operates under the auspices of a unified energy-intelligence, the name of which is the Endless Light. Even in this violent, transitory, tumultuous sphere of illusion, there is an all-embracing aspect of harmony, peace, and unanimity with which each of us can connect.

Universal Unfolding

The upper lights cannot descend to their proper Vessels until the lower Vessels have unfolded and evolved so as to permit the lower lights to become enclothed by their respective Vessels. This means that until *Nefesh*, the lowest level of spiritual existence, has reached the level of *Malchut*, where it is made manifest in the physical world, none of the higher lights can attain their proper Vessels.

The paradox we find in this process, whereby the lofty and elevated must wait for the lowly, is a profound expression of the essential duality of the universe. And this paradox answers the question relating to the nature of the levels of spirituality that have existed through the ages, culminating in our age, which is called the Age of Messiah.

Our generation represents the lowest and final vessel of the phase of *Malchut*. Yet it is by virtue of the appearance of this lowly vessel that the lights of *Nefesh* can finally achieve their appointed place. In so doing, a vacuum is created in the upper vessels, allowing the upper lights to be drawn down. This is the character of our age, where manifestations of the lowest level of spirituality are revealed in the existence of so many material-oriented, pleasure-seeking, nonspiritual people. Yet at the same time, we witness the reawakening of spirituality among the young as well as advances in the world of science that threaten to destroy all our established concepts of order and purpose.

Our generation will bear witness to the perfect understanding that results from the complete union of the Lights with their appointed Vessels.

The Zohar promises that with the ushering in of the Age of Aquarius, the cosmos will become readily accessible to human understanding. It states that "the gates of wisdom above and the rivers of wisdom below will open up" (*Zohar I*, 117a).

We can and must regain control of our lives and environment. To achieve this objective, Kabbalah provides us with an opportunity to transcend the crushing weight of universal negativity.

The Age of Aquarius will pressure those whose life pursuits are for momentary pleasure into an astonishing realization that the good life of permanency is theirs for the asking. A clear understanding of our cosmos will dictate that happiness, energy, and peace of mind operate in a manner similar to a light bulb. The stronger the desire of the negative pole, the greater the necessity for the filament to restrict this fulfillment — for only then is the reality of circuitry achieved.

Through the circular concept, it becomes possible to convert the desire to receive into a desire to impart, transmuting, we might say, the letter "M" in "me" to the letter "W" in "we." The "M" points downward, emphasizing the connection with the physical world, while the "W" reaches up toward the heavens, the Creator. Through this affinity of desires, we are brought closer to the structure of the Creator's desire to impart and can free ourselves from the stigma of being able to receive only for ourselves. From our earthly existence, we are led to a higher spiritual level of consciousness, to liberation from the tyranny of the five senses, and to a higher realm of spiritual existence.

In the Messianic Age, much will change as a result of a simple conversion of energy. The desire to receive for oneself alone will be converted into the Desire to Receive for the Sake of Sharing. Thus, the fraction of reality now obscured by illusion will disappear. For some, that age is here today. For those who understand and exercise the principle of resistance in their daily lives, the illusion of darkness holds little sway. The objective, then, for kabbalists, is to achieve an altered state of consciousness in which they can remove the illusion and again unveil the Light.

More Books that can bring the wisdom of Kabbalah into your life

Wheels of a Soul
By Rav Berg

In *Wheels of a Soul,* Kabbalist Rav Berg reveals the keys to answering these and many more questions that lie at the heart of our existence as human beings. Specifically, Rav Berg explains why we must acknowledge and explore the lives we have already lived in order to understand the life we are living today . . .

Make no mistake: you have been here before. Reincarnation is a fact— and just as science is now beginning to recognize that time and space may be nothing but illusions, Rav Berg shows why death itself is the greatest illusion of all.

In this book you learn much more than the answers to these questions. You will understand your true purpose in the world and discover tools to identify your life's soul mate. Read *Wheels of a Soul* and let one of the greatest kabbalistic masters of our time change your life forever.

The Power of You
By Rav Berg

For the past 5,000 years, neither science nor psychology has been able to solve the fundamental problem of chaos in people's lives.

Now, one man is providing the answer. He is Kabbalist Rav Berg.

Beneath the pain and chaos that disrupts our lives, Kabbalist Rav Berg brings to light a hidden realm of order, purpose, and unity. Revealed is a universe in which mind becomes master over matter—a world in which God, human thought, and the entire cosmos are mysteriously interconnected.

Join this generation's premier kabbalist on a mind-bending journey along the cutting edge of reality. Peer into the vast reservoir of spiritual wisdom that is Kabbalah, where the secrets of creation, life, and death have remained hidden for thousands of years.

The Red String: The Power of Protection
By Yehuda Berg

Read the book that everyone is wearing!

Discover the ancient technology that empowers and fuels the hugely popular Red String, the most widely recognized tool of kabbalistic wisdom. Yehuda Berg, author of the international best-seller *The 72 Names of God: Technology for the Soul*, continues to reveal the secrets of the world's oldest and most powerful wisdom with his new book, *The Red String: The Power of Protection*. Discover the antidote to the negative effects of the dreaded "Evil Eye" in this second book of the Technology for the Soul series.

Find out the real power behind the Red String and why millions of people won't leave home without it.

It's all here. Everything you wanted to know about the Red String but were afraid to ask!

The Dreams Book: Finding Your Way in the Dark
By Yehuda Berg

 In *The Dreams Book*, the debut installment of the Technology for the Soul Series, national best-selling author Yehuda Berg lifts the curtain of reality to reveal secrets of dream interpretation that have remained hidden for centuries.

Readers will discover a millennia-old system for understanding dreams and will learn powerful techniques to help them find soul mates, discover career opportunities, be alerted to potential illness in the body, improve relationships with others, develop an overall deeper awareness, and much more.

The dream state is a mysterious and fascinating realm in which the rules of reality do not apply. This book is the key to navigating the dreamscape, where the answers to all of life's questions await.

187

Becoming Like God
By Michael Berg

At the age of 16, kabbalistic scholar Michael Berg began the herculean task of translating *The Zohar*, Kabbalah's chief text, from its original Aramaic into its first complete English translation. *The Zohar*, which consists of 23 volumes, is considered a compendium of virtually all information pertaining to the universe, and its wisdom is only beginning to be verified today.

During the ten years he worked on *The Zohar*, Michael Berg discovered the long-lost secret for which humanity has searched for more than 5,000 years: how to achieve our ultimate destiny. *Becoming Like God* reveals the transformative method by which people can actually break free of what is called "ego nature" to achieve total joy and lasting life.

Berg puts forth the revolutionary idea that for the first time in history, an opportunity is being made available to humankind: an opportunity to Become Like God.

The Zohar

"Bringing *The Zohar* from near oblivion to wide accessibility has taken many decades. It is an achievement of which we are truly proud and grateful."

—Michael Berg

Composed more than 2,000 years ago, *The Zohar* is a set of 23 books, a commentary on biblical and spiritual matters in the form of conversations among spiritual masters. But to describe *The Zohar* only in physical terms is greatly misleading. In truth, *The Zohar* is nothing less than a powerful tool for achieving the most important purposes of our lives. It was given to all humankind by the Creator to bring us protection, to connect us with the Creator's Light, and ultimately to fulfill our birthright of true spiritual transformation.

Eighty years ago, when The Kabbalah Centre was founded, *The Zohar* had virtually disappeared from the world. Few people in the general population had ever heard of it. Whoever sought to read it—in any country, in any language, at any price—faced a long and futile search. Today all this has changed. Through the work of The Kabbalah Centre and the editorial efforts of Michael Berg, *The Zohar* is now being brought to the world, not only in the original Aramaic language but also in English.

The new English *Zohar* provides everything for connecting to this sacred text on all levels: the original Aramaic text for scanning; an English translation; and clear, concise commentary for study and learning.

189

The Kabbalah Centre

The International Leader in the Education of Kabbalah

Since its founding, The Kabbalah Centre has had a single mission: to improve and transform people's lives by bringing the power and wisdom of Kabbalah to all who wish to partake of it.

Through the lifelong efforts of Rav Berg, his wife Karen, and the great spiritual lineage of which they are a part, an astonishing 3.5 million people around the world have already been touched by the powerful teachings of Kabbalah. And each year, the numbers are growing!

As the leading source of kabbalistic wisdom with 50 locations around the world, The Kabbalah Centre offers you a wealth of resources, including:

• The English *Zohar*, the first-ever comprehensive English translation of the foundation of kabbalistic wisdom. In 23 beautifully bound volumes, this edition includes the full Aramaic text, the English translation, and detailed commentary, making this once-inaccessible text understandable to all.

• A full schedule of workshops, lectures, and evening classes for students at all levels of knowledge and experience.

- CDs, audiotapes, videotapes, and books in English and ten other languages.

- One of the Internet's most exciting and comprehensive websites, www.kabbalah.com—which receives more than 100,000 visitors each month.

- A constantly expanding list of events and publications to help you live the teachings of Kabbalah with greater understanding and excitement.

Discover why The Kabbalah Centre is one of the world's fastest-growing spiritual organizations. Our sole purpose is to improve people's lives through the teachings of Kabbalah. Let us show you what Kabbalah can do for you!

Each Kabbalah Centre location hosts free introductory lectures. For more information on Kabbalah or on these and other products and services, call 1-800-KABBALAH.

Wherever you are, there's a Kabbalah Centre—because now you can call 1-800-KABBALAH from almost anywhere, 18 hours a day, and get answers or guidance right over the telephone. You'll be connected to distinguished senior faculty who are on hand to help you understand Kabbalah as deeply as you want to—whether it involves recommending a course of study; deciding which books/tapes to take or the order in which to take them; discussing the material; or anything else you wish to know about Kabbalah.

This book is dedicated to all of our loving guides in life, like my teacher Eliyahu, who has taught me how to truly give and share.

Thank you to my friends and family for introducing me to the love and care I experience at The Kabbalah Centre. I am grateful to be part of the legacy of those who are transforming the world.

May everyone take the time for reflection in order to allow all of the Light to come into our hearts and souls.

Tim Krass